Healthy Pescatarian Meals Featuring Seafood and Vegetarian Proteins

EAT MEAT WITHOUT FEET

165 RECIPES

BY CARRIE SHAPLEY

Fried Fish Sandwich, recipe on page 37

Copyright © 2022 by Carrie Shapley

All rights reserved. This book may not be reproduced or stored in whole or in part by any means without the written permission of the author except for brief quotations for the purpose of review.

First Edition

ISBN: 978-1-957723-67-9 (hard cover)
       978-1-957723-66-2 (soft cover)

Shapley. Carrie.

Published by Warren Publishing
Charlotte, NC
www.warrenpublishing.net
Printed in the United States

For Aunt Sallie, the best fairy godmother anyone could have.

Quick Macaroni and Cheese, recipe on page 59

INTRODUCTION

I think, deep down, I've always been a pescatarian. I grew up during a time when TV dinners were new, meatloaf was king, and I was supposed to be grateful for slabs of meat on the table for dinner. But I wasn't. I hated steak, I ate pork chops in the tiniest bites possible and then washed them down with gallons of milk, I cringed when my mother announced we were having venison for dinner, and I wasn't all that crazy about chicken. I was a kid, so I didn't have the language or experience to articulate what I liked, what I wanted, what I craved. But I do now.

I love fish. I love any morsel of meat that comes out of a shell. I love cheese and eggs and nuts and beans of every sort. I even love tofu. And as luck would have it, eating those things instead of meat with feet has been good for my body. Once my husband and I switched for good to a pescatarian diet, our "bad" cholesterol dropped precipitously – his by sixty points.

We tried and succeeded at being vegetarians for awhile over concerns about over-fishing of wild populations. But more careful, well-informed purchasing brought us back to seafood, as the balance of a pescatarian diet just felt right for us. We like the incredible variety a pescatarian diet has, and we reap the health benefits of both a plant-based diet and a diet rich in omega-3 oils.

The recipes in this cookbook are detailed, so the dishes can be prepared by novice and experienced cooks alike. And they employ ingredients you will be able to find in your local grocery store.

I love to cook. I love to cook for myself and for others. I love teaching and inspiring others to get into the kitchen and whip stuff up. I hope that my love of and enthusiasm for creativity in the kitchen comes through in the contents of this book. And most of all, I hope you will slip on an apron and give one of my recipes a go!

White Pizza, recipe on page 52

TABLE OF CONTENTS

EGG ENTREES	1
Breakfast Burrito	2
Crab Deviled Eggs	3
Creamed Spinach with Eggs on Top	4
Egg Casserole with Cheese Sauce	5
Egg Salad	6
"Ham"-and-Egg Cups	7
Quiche	8
Shakshuka	10
Strata	11
Tex-Mex Breakfast Casserole	12

SOUPS, STEWS, AND CHILI	13
Brazilian Feijoada	14
Chili	15
Creamy Chik'n Noodle Soup	16
Gumbo	17
Indian Stew	18
Lentil-Barley Stew	19
Mixed Bean Soup	20
Seafood Chowder	21
Smoked Salmon Stew	22
Spicy Lentil Soup	23
Split Pea Soup	24
Tarascan Indian Soup	25
White Bean Soup	26

MAIN DISH SALADS	27
Crab Cobb Salad	28
Greek Tortellini Pasta Salad	29
Smoked Salmon and Goat Cheese Salad	30
Tabbouleh Salad with Shrimp	31
Thai Cold Noodle Salad	32

BURGERS AND SANDWICHES 33
- Chick'n Caesar Wrap 34
- Crab Wrap 35
- Cram Cakes 36
- Fried Fish Sandwich 37
- Falafel 38
- Lentil Burgers 40
- Nut Burgers 41
- Salmon Patties 42
- Seafood Salad 43
- Spicy Black Bean Burgers 44

PIZZA 45
- Chicago-Style Deep Dish Pizza 46
- Calzones 48
- Margherita Pizza 49
- Mexican Pizza 50
- Sicilian Pizza 51
- White Pizza 52

QUICK AND EASY ENTREES 53
- 30-Minute Chili 54
- Baked Lemon-Garlic Fish 55
- Creamy Pesto Orzo with Shrimp 56
- Garlic Shrimp 57
- Kielbasa and Potatoes 58
- Quick Macaroni and Cheese 59
- Salmon with Honey-Mustard Glaze 60
- Shrimp Fried Rice 61
- Sloppy Joes 62
- Tony Macaroni 63
- Wasabi Tuna Steaks 64

FISH ENTREES 65
- Beer Battered Fish 66
- Fish Curry 67
- Fish Tacos with Kimchi Slaw 68
- Fish Sticks 70
- Marinated Salmon 71
- Salmon Alfredo 72
- Salmon Ceviche 73
- Tuna-Rice Delight 73
- Salmon Quiche 74
- Spinach and Feta Stuffed Salmon 75
- Swordfish Kebabs 76
- Tilapia Stuffed with Lobster 77
- Tuscan Stuffed Mahi Mahi 78

SHELLFISH ENTREES 79
- Clams in White Sauce with Linguini 80
- Coconut Shrimp 81
- Coconut-Lime Shrimp 82
- Crab Egg Rolls 83
- Crab Quiche 84
- Fried Oysters 85
- Lobster Mac-n-Cheese 86
- Mussels 87
- Scallops and Gnocchi in Cream Sauce 88
- Seafood Newburg 89
- Seafood Lasagna 90
- Shrimp Fajitas 92

VEGETARIAN ENTREES 93
- Bibimbap 94
- Biscuits and Sausage Gravy 96
- Black Bean Burrito Bowls 97
- Chik'n Pot Pie 98
- Eggplant Parmigiana 100
- "Ham" and Scalloped Potatoes 101
- Indian "Meat" Balls in Coconut Curry Sauce 102
- Lasagna 104
- Macaroni and Cheese 106
- Mostaccioli 107
- Shepherd's Pie 108
- Stroganoff 109
- Stuffed Peppers 110
- Swiss Macaroni and Cheese 111
- Taco Casserole 112
- Salsa Beans 112

VEGAN ENTREES 113
- Dolmades (Stuffed Grape Leaves) 114
- Masala Peanuts 115
- Spaghetti with Roasted Vegetable Sauce 116
- Stir-fry with Spicy Peanut Sauce 117
- Sweet-and-Sour 118
- Swellington Wellington 119
- Vegan Macaroni and Cheese 120

SIDE DISHES — 121
- "Bacon" Onion Rings — 122
- Cornbread Stuffing — 123
- Cornbread — 124
- Vegan Cornbread — 125
- Creamy Coleslaw — 126
- Fancy Rice — 127
- Focaccia — 128
- Fried Green Tomatoes — 129
- Hush Puppies — 130
- Irish Soda Bread — 131
- Lemon Orzo — 132
- Marinated Vegetables — 133
- Mashed Potatoes — 134
- Mexican Grain Salad — 136
- Mexican Rice — 137
- Pasta Salad — 138
- Potato Salad — 139
- Quinoa with Raisins and Pepitas — 140
- Sweet Potato Fries — 140
- Refried Beans — 141
- Scones — 142
- Thanksgiving Sage-Onion Stuffing — 143
- Vegan Baked Beans — 144

DRY RUBS AND SEASONINGS — 145
- Cajun Rub — 146
- Hot Mustard Rub — 146
- Chinese 12-Spice Rub — 146
- Indian Rub — 147
- Texas Rub — 147
- Berbere Seasoning — 148
- Curry Powder — 148
- Greek Seasoning — 149
- Italian Seasoning — 149
- Seasoned Salt — 150
- Simon and Garfunkel Seasoning — 150
- Garam Masala — 151
- Taco Seasoning — 151

SALAD DRESSINGS — 152
- Avocado Salad Dressing — 153
- Basil Vinaigrette — 153
- Bleu Cheese Salad Dressing — 153
- Caesar Salad Dressing — 154
- Cranberry-Lemon Vinaigrette — 154
- Greek Vinaigrette — 155
- Italian Vinaigrette — 155
- Lemon Vinaigrette — 156
- Raspberry Vinaigrette — 156
- Ranch Salad Dressing — 156
- Thai Ginger Vinaigrette — 157
- Thousand Island Salad Dressing — 157

DIPPING SAUCES — 158
- Cilantro Pesto — 159
- Chipotle Aioli — 159
- Pesto Sauce — 160
- Hoisin Sauce — 160
- Pizza Sauce — 161
- Salsa Verde — 161
- Sweet-and-Sour Sauce #1 — 162
- Sweet-and-Sour Sauce #2 — 162
- Skordalia — 162
- Tartar Sauce — 163
- Toum — 163
- Tzatziki Sauce — 163
- Artichoke Dipping Sauce — 164
- Seafood Cocktail Sauce — 164

Shakshuka, recipe on page 10

EGG ENTREES

My three desert-island foods (If you were stranded on a desert island, what three foods would you want with you?) are potatoes, eggs, and cheese. It would pain me to leave mushrooms off the list, but desert islands have moist caves full of them, right?

It should not surprise you, then, to learn that this is one of my favorite chapters in this book. Other chapters may have a few recipes in them that I make only occasionally, but the recipes here are ones I make All. The. Time. And, word to the wise: eggs are not just for breakfast, and even if you think they are, breakfast is delicious any time of day.

BREAKFAST BURRITO

Serves 1

This way of making a breakfast burrito is both faster to make and easier to eat than those made by traditional methods. Fantastic for a quick breakfast-to-go!

Ingredients

- 2 tsp. vegetable oil, divided
- ½ to 1 cup of your desired fixings (vegetarian sausage or bacon, canned beans, sliced fresh vegetables, leftover vegetables, etc.)
- 2 eggs, beaten
- 1 pinch salt
- 1 whole grain 8" tortilla (double all ingredients if using a burrito-size tortilla)
- 1 oz. sliced or shredded cheese (¼ cup)

Directions

1. In an 8" frying pan, heat 1 teaspoon of oil over medium heat.
2. Add your desired fixings and sauté until cooked and hot. Stir almost constantly.
3. Add the remaining teaspoon of oil to the pan. Stir or swirl pan to distribute oil.
4. Add eggs to pan, distributing evenly. Sprinkle with salt.
5. Lay tortilla on top of everything. Press it down gently so it sticks in the raw portions of egg.
6. When the bottom layer of egg is cooked, flip the whole mess over. If toppings scatter, scoop them back on top of the tortilla.
7. Cook until the tortilla is lightly browned, and the eggs are cooked. Move to a plate.
8. Top cooked eggs with cheese and any condiments you desire (hot sauce, diced avocado, salsa, or other). Roll up and eat.

CRAB DEVILED EGGS

Makes 24 egg halves

If you are a deviled-egg lover or have invited some over for brunch, it would not be over-kill to double this recipe. In my experience, I find I need to run quite a few "quality checks" while making them and transferring them to a serving platter. And if I have "helpers" in the kitchen … well, they usually feel a need to corroborate my findings.

Ingredients

Eggs:

- 12 large or extra large eggs

Filling:

- 6 oz. package smoky tempeh or other vegetarian bacon
- ⅓ cup mayonnaise
- 6 oz. can lump crab meat, drained, or 4 oz. lump crab meat
- 1 tsp. brown or Dijon-style mustard
- 1 tsp. Old Bay Seasoning

Directions

1. **For Eggs:** Hard-boil eggs by placing them in a 3-quart saucepan. Cover eggs with cold water to a depth 1" over their tops.
2. Place pot over medium-high heat and bring to a boil.
3. Cover pot, turn burner off, and let pot sit on burner for 15 minutes.
4. Drain hot water off eggs and replace with cold water. Let eggs sit until completely cooled, replacing water with fresh, cold water if needed.
5. **For Bacon:** While eggs are cooking and cooling, cook bacon until browned and crisp according to package instructions.
6. Transfer bacon to a cutting board and chop finely.
7. When eggs are cool, crack shells and peel eggs. Rinse any stray bits of shell off eggs.
8. **For Filling:** Cut eggs in half, lengthwise.
9. Remove yolks and place them in a small mixing bowl. Add mayonnaise and smash yolks with the tines of a fork to break them into small pieces. Mix until no big lumps of yolk remain.
10. Add chopped bacon, crab, mustard, and seasoning to yolk mixture. Stir until mixture is creamy and homogenous.
11. Lay egg white halves on a plate or platter. Fill cavities of eggs with crab-yolk mixture, mounding filling up a bit, and using all of it. Serve deviled eggs chilled.

CREAMED SPINACH WITH EGGS ON TOP

Serves 4

Eggs prepared this way are amazing! One of my favorite ways to make eggs "fancy," this recipe is simple and straightforward, but the results look and taste like I fussed. Complex flavors satisfy your tastebuds, while visually, the eggs sit all prim and proper atop a luxurious bed of green.

Ingredients

- 2 Tbsp. butter
- 1 Tbsp. vegetable oil
- 2 cups finely minced white or yellow onion (1 large onion)
- 1 Tbsp. finely minced or pressed garlic (3 large cloves)
- 32 oz. frozen, chopped spinach (three 10 oz. boxes or two 16 oz. bags), thawed but not drained
- 2 tsp. salt
- ¼ tsp. ground black pepper
- 1 cup heavy cream
- 8 oz. shredded provolone, swiss, gruyere, or Italian blend cheese (2 cups)
- 8 eggs
- 2 pinches salt

Directions

1. Preheat oven to 400°.
2. In a 10" oven-proof frying pan, melt the butter and oil together over medium-high heat.
3. Add the onion and garlic. Sauté for 2 minutes until the onion is translucent.
4. Add the spinach, salt, and pepper. Stir the mixture to combine. Cook until moisture is reduced by half (about 5 minutes).
5. Add heavy cream and cheese. Cook, stirring almost constantly, until cheese melts and mixture begins to bubble.
6. Turn heat off. Make 8 deep depressions in the spinach mixture and crack an egg into each one. Sprinkle eggs lightly with salt.
7. Place pan in oven and bake eggs for 15 (for runny yolks) to 20 (for cooked yolks) minutes. The whites of the eggs will be opaque when cooked.

EGG CASSEROLE WITH CHEESE SAUCE

Makes one 9" x 13" pan; serves 6-8 as a main course or 12 as part of a brunch buffet

This is my go-to dish for Easter brunch. It is tasty, holds well on a buffet, and in a pinch, it can be made the night before (the eggs in the bottom of the pan will discolor slightly, but I've never had anyone complain, especially after tasting!). Besides all that, it has three of my all-time favorite things in it: cheese, eggs, and mushrooms.

Ingredients

Cheese Sauce:

- 2 Tbsp. butter
- 3 Tbsp. all-purpose flour
- 2 cups milk
- 1 ½ cups shredded cheese (6 oz.), cheddar or swiss is best
- ⅓ cup grated Parmesan cheese
- 2 Tbsp. dry white wine (Sauvignon Blanc or Pinot Grigio)
- ½ tsp. seasoned salt

Veggies:

- 2 Tbsp. butter
- 16 oz. sliced fresh mushrooms (about 6 cups)
- 1 bunch green onions, sliced (about 1 ½ cups)

Eggs:

- 4 Tbsp. butter
- 24 eggs, beaten
- 1 tsp. salt
- ¼ tsp. ground black pepper

Garnish:

- 1 Tbsp. snipped chives (dried or fresh)

Directions

1. **For Cheese Sauce:** In 1-quart saucepan over medium heat, melt butter.
2. Add flour to make a roux and stir until no white spots of flour remain. Cook for 1 minute, stirring constantly.
3. Add milk and stir with a whisk to eliminate lumps.
4. Cook until mixture is boiling and thickened, stirring occasionally.
5. Add cheeses, wine, and salt. Reduce heat to low and stir until cheese is melted.
6. Remove from heat. Sauce may be made up to a week in advance of assembly of this dish (cover and refrigerate sauce until needed).
7. **For Veggies:** In a large frying pan over medium heat, melt butter. Sauté mushrooms and onions until mushrooms are barely cooked (5–10 minutes).
8. Transfer veggie mixture to a bowl and set aside.
9. Preheat oven to 350°.
10. **For Eggs:** In the same frying pan used for the veggies, melt half the butter. Scramble half the eggs with half the salt and pepper.
11. **To Assemble Dish:** Transfer the dozen scrambled eggs to the bottom of a 9" x 13" baking pan, spreading them to an even thickness.
12. Top eggs with the veggies, distributing evenly.
13. Return frying pan to burner. Melt remaining butter and scramble remaining eggs with remaining salt and pepper.
14. Spread cooked eggs over the veggies and spoon the cheese sauce over all.
15. Sprinkle chives on top (This dish may be prepared to this point ahead of time. Cover and refrigerate).
16. Bake, uncovered, for 20–30 minutes. Serve hot.

EGG SALAD

Makes 2 cups

Egg salad is one of those things you can eat pretty much any way you please: in a sandwich, on a cracker, straight from the bowl with a big spoon, scooped up with sliced fresh veggies, and the list goes on. I am old-school about my egg salad, so this recipe will yield a classic, simple, straightforward bowl of familiar.

Ingredients

- 6 large eggs
- ⅓ cup mayonnaise
- 2 Tbsp. sweet pickle relish
- 1 tsp. Dijon-style mustard
- ¼ tsp. ground celery seed
- ¼ tsp. salt

Directions

1. Hard-boil eggs (directions on page 3, if needed).
2. When eggs are cool, crack shells and peel eggs. Rinse any stray bits of shell off eggs.
3. Chop hard-boiled eggs and add to a medium mixing bowl.
4. Add remaining ingredients and stir well.
5. Taste, adjust seasonings, and chill until serving time.

"HAM"-AND-EGG CUPS

Makes 12 muffin-sized cups; serves 4-6

Quick and convenient! Great to make ahead for breakfasts on-the-go. And if you want to make a variety of these for brunch or for family breakfasts for the week ahead, try making some with a spoon of salsa under the egg and pepper jack cheese on top, or make some with leftover veggies tossed in, or make some with sliced olives under the eggs and feta cheese on top, or make some ... You get the idea!

Ingredients

- 5.5 oz. package vegetarian ham slices (12 slices)
- 2 Tbsp. snipped fresh or dried chives
- 12 large eggs
- 1 tsp. seasoned salt
- 8 oz. shredded cheese, your choice of: cheddar, swiss, Mexican blend, or Italian blend (2 cups)

Directions

1. Preheat oven to 375°.
2. Lightly grease a standard 12-cup muffin tin.
3. Place one slice of veggie ham in each of the cups, pressing the ham into the cavity to form a cup.
4. Sprinkle ½ tsp. chives in each ham cup.
5. Crack one egg into each ham cup. Sprinkle the top of each egg with a pinch of salt.
6. Top each cup with 2 Tbsp. grated cheese.
7. Bake for 15 minutes until eggs are firm, and cheese is lightly browned. Serve hot.

QUICHE

Serves 4-6

I make quiche all the time. It is quick to whip together, lends itself to endless improvisation, and is a great way to use up fiddly bits of things left from making other dishes. And if you skip making a from-scratch pie crust and either buy a ready-made crust or go crustless, it comes together even faster.

Ingredients

Crust:

- 9" unbaked pie crust (store-bought or homemade from recipe on page 98), optional

Filling:

- 4 jumbo or 5 large eggs
- 1 cup sour cream or plain Greek yogurt or plain yogurt or milk
- 2 Tbsp. all-purpose flour
- ½ tsp. seasoned salt
- 2 cups of whatever seafood, vegetarian meat, or veggies you choose (dice or slice and pre-cook everything except tomatoes and green onions)
- 1 cup diced or grated cheese (4 oz.)

Directions

1. Make crust. If making quiche crustless, grease a 9" pie plate and set aside.
2. Preheat oven to 375°.
3. In a large mixing bowl, beat together eggs, sour cream, flour, and salt with a whisk until mixture is smooth and homogenous.
4. With a spoon or rubber spatula, fold in the meats, veggies, and/or cheeses of your choice.
5. Transfer mixture to the prepared pie crust or pie plate.
6. Bake for 45 minutes.
7. When quiche is done, the top will be dry, not shiny, and the center will not jiggle. Slice into wedges and serve.
8. Quiche may be made ahead and frozen (after baking). To serve, thaw quiche, cover with aluminum foil, and reheat in a 300° oven for 20 minutes.

Excellent Quiche Combinations:

Greek

- 14 oz. can artichoke hearts, drained and cut in thin wedges
- ¼ cup diced red onion or thinly sliced green onion
- ½ cup diced fresh tomatoes or halved cherry tomatoes
- ½ cup sliced black olives
- ¼ tsp. dried oregano
- 1 cup crumbled feta cheese (4 oz.)

Asparagus / Spinach

- 1 bunch asparagus, rinsed, cut in 1" pieces and cooked al dente or 10 oz. package frozen, chopped spinach, thawed and drained
- 5 oz. package vegetarian bacon, roughly diced and pan-fried in 1 Tbsp. olive oil
- 1 Tbsp. snipped chives (fresh or dried)
- 1 cup grated or diced swiss or provolone cheese (4 oz.)

Broccoli

- 1 large head broccoli, cut in small pieces and cooked al dente
- 4 oz. can mushrooms, drained
- 1 cup grated or diced cheddar cheese (4 oz.)

Sausage-Onion

- 2 cups sliced onions, slowly sautéed in 1 Tbsp. vegetable oil until caramelized
- 6–8 links vegetarian breakfast sausage, pan-fried in 1 Tbsp. vegetable oil, then sliced
- 1 cup grated or diced Asiago or gouda cheese (4 oz.)

Zucchini

- 2 small zucchini, cut in ½" dice and cooked al dente
- 4 oz. fresh mushrooms (any variety), sliced and cooked al dente
- 2 Tbsp. snipped chives (fresh or dried)
- 1 cup shredded Italian 6-cheese blend (4 oz.)

Seafood

- 1 cup cooked shrimp, diced
- 6 oz. can crab meat, drained
- 2 Tbsp. snipped chives (fresh or dried)
- 1 cup grated or diced mozzarella, swiss, fontina, or gouda cheese

SHAKSHUKA
Serves 4-6

Shakshuka is an egg dish that originated in northern Africa and is now common across the Middle East. It is, quite simply, a poached egg casserole with a zesty tomato sauce on the bottom and a healthy dose of feta cheese on top. You can make the tomato sauce ahead of time to save time in the morning, or you can do what I do and serve this for dinner.

Ingredients

Spice Blend:
- 1 tsp. ground coriander
- 1 tsp. paprika (sweet, not hot)
- 1 tsp. salt
- ½ tsp. ground black pepper
- ½ tsp. chili powder
- ¼ tsp. ground cinnamon
- ⅛ tsp. red pepper flakes

Sauce:
- 2 Tbsp. olive or vegetable oil
- 1 large yellow or white onion, diced (about 2 cups)
- 1 red bell pepper, seeded and diced (about 2 cups)
- 6 large cloves garlic, finely minced or pressed (2 Tbsp.)
- 28 oz. can diced tomatoes
- 1 Tbsp. tomato paste

Eggs:
- 8 large eggs
- ½ tsp. salt

Topping:
- 4 oz. crumbled feta cheese (1 cup)
- 1 Tbsp. dried parsley

Directions

1. In a small ramekin or mug, combine ingredients for spice blend. Set by side of cooktop.
2. Preheat oven to 400°.
3. **For Sauce:** In a 10–12" diameter, deep, oven-safe skillet over medium-high heat, place oil.
4. When oil is hot, add onion, pepper, and garlic. Stir and sauté until onion is translucent (about 5 minutes).
5. Add spice blend to onion mixture and continue cooking until spices are fragrant (about 1 minute).
6. Add tomatoes and tomato paste, stir, and heat sauce to boiling.
7. Reduce heat to low and simmer sauce for 15 minutes, stirring occasionally.
8. Turn heat off.
9. With the back of a spoon, make a deep depression in the sauce for each of the eggs. Crack each egg into a depression. Sprinkle eggs with salt.
10. Place pan in oven and bake eggs for 10 (for runny yolks) to 15 (for cooked yolks) minutes. The whites of eggs will be opaque when cooked.
11. Remove pan from oven and sprinkle feta and parsley on top. Serve hot.

Shakshuka is pictured on page 1.

STRATA

Makes 9" x 13" pan

Strata is one of those things that cannot easily be quantified into a recipe because it is a this-and-that, here's-what-I-have-to-work-with sort of thing. In general, it is an egg casserole made in a 9" x 13" baking pan, with slices of buttered bread on the bottom (buttered side down), a combination of meats, veggies, and cheese in the middle, slices of buttered bread on top (buttered side up), and an egg mixture poured over the whole thing. Certain things are important:

Good Combinations of Fillings:

- 1 lb. veggie sausage + 2 cups onions + 1 cup green bell pepper + 2 cups shredded cheddar cheese (8 oz.)
- two 6 oz. packages vegetarian bacon + 8 oz. sliced mushrooms + 1 cup onions + 8 oz. package 6-cheese Italian blend

Guidelines

1. The casserole must be assembled at least 8 hours before baking to allow the egg mixture to fully absorb into the bread. If you are using a nice, sturdy bread, overnight won't be enough, and you should plan on making the Strata 24 hours ahead. This is a selling feature of the recipe (you can make it the day before company arrives).
2. For a 9" x 13" pan made up with ¾" slices of good French bread, use 12 eggs + 2 cups milk + 1 tsp. salt + pinch black pepper. If making a smaller pan or using cheap, wimpy bread, adjust amounts accordingly.
3. Season the egg mixture and any cooked veggies with salt and pepper.
4. Herbs of your choosing may be added to the mix.
5. I like adding 1 or 2 cloves of smashed garlic to the butter used in buttering the bread (about 4 Tbsp. butter + 2 cloves garlic).
6. Cheese is essential, but meats and veggies aren't.
7. Pre-cook any meats and most any vegetables you use (green onions and tomatoes being about the only exceptions).
8. Bake uncovered for about 45 minutes in a preheated 375° oven (the top should be golden brown, and the egg mixture should appear cooked and dry).
9. When cooked, cut the Strata into 3" squares (+/-) and serve.

TEX-MEX BREAKFAST CASSEROLE

Serves 6-10

This slow-cooker casserole is just the loveliest thing to quickly dump together before bed. Set the slow-cooker on "low," and you will wake to the most delicious aromas and a company-worthy hot breakfast. All the flavor of huevos rancheros without the fuss, you can customize your level of heat with the salsa and cheese you choose.

Ingredients

Casserole:

- 3 lbs. potatoes, scrubbed and cut in ¾" dice (about 8 fist-sized spuds–do not peel)
- 12 oz. package vegetarian chorizo (soy or seitan), sliced or crumbled
- 15 oz. can black beans, drained and rinsed
- 16 oz. jar salsa (2 cups), your choice of heat levels
- 16 oz. package shredded cheese (4 cups): mozzarella, queso fresco, or cheddar for a mild casserole; pepper Jack for medium spiciness; and Cabot Creamery's Habanero Cheddar for intense heat
- 12 eggs
- 1 cup milk
- 2 tsp. salt
- ¼ tsp. ground black pepper

Serving:

- 1 cup salsa
- 1 cup sour cream

Directions

1. In ceramic liner of a large slow-cooker, deposit half the diced potatoes and spread to an even thickness.
2. Top them with the chorizo, beans, salsa, and half the cheese, distributing each evenly.
3. Lay remaining potatoes on top and sprinkle the rest of the cheese over all.
4. In a medium mixing bowl, whisk together the eggs, milk, salt, and pepper.
5. Pour egg mixture over top of the layers in the slow-cooker.
6. Place lid on slow-cooker. Cook casserole for 8 hours on low or 4 hours on high.
7. Dish up by scooping down through layers of casserole. Serve with salsa and sour cream on the side.

Gumbo, recipe on page 17

SOUPS, STEWS, AND CHILI

My grandparents lived on a farm, and my grandfather's favorite lunch was a bowl of hearty soup and a slice of pie. So my grandmother made soup and pie all the time. She probably had a larger repertoire, but as a kid, I only remember three kinds of soup coming out of her kitchen: beef, chicken noodle, and vegetable with dry beans. All of which were perfection — grass-fed beef from a neighbor's farm, homemade noodles, and vegetables fresh from the garden.

My grandmother's pie repertoire was a different matter. I can count nine kinds of pie she made with regularity — apple, blueberry, peach, cherry, rhubarb, pecan, pumpkin, mincemeat, and banana cream. When local fruits were in season, she would make a batch of pies, wrap them, lay them out to freeze, and then stack them in a chest freezer. This sounds crazy, but I adored that freezer. Sometimes, I would wander off just to sneak a peek at those stacks and stacks of pies.

Despite the fact that I don't cook like my grandmother, I think of her often when I am at work in the kitchen. I use her crust recipe when I make pie, I make meals because they are someone else's favorite, and I make soup from scratch because it just tastes better.

BRAZILIAN FEIJOADA

Serves 6-8

Considered the "National Dish of Brazil," this stew is typically packed with meat. Our friends from Brazil made a decidedly nonvegetarian version of this dish for our circle of friends many, many times, and I loved the flavors but not all that meat. This vegan version retains those authentic flavors while packing a surprisingly "meaty" punch by employing meat-free sausage and chicken. The Brazilian way to serve this dish is with a side of cooked greens (collard or kale) and a plate of sliced oranges.

Ingredients

Beans:

- 1 lb. black beans
- water for soaking
- 4 cups vegetable broth or 4 cups water + 1 Tbsp. vegetable bouillon
- 12 oz. package vegan chorizo or kielbasa, sliced ½" thick
- 1 large white or yellow onion diced (about 2 cups)
- 1 green bell pepper, seeded and diced (about 1 ½ cups)
- 4 oz. can diced green chilies (or 1 jalapeño pepper, with seeds, finely minced)
- 3 large cloves garlic, finely minced or pressed (1 Tbsp.)
- 2 bay leaves
- 2 tsp. ground coriander
- 1 tsp. dried epazote (Mexican oregano) or dried oregano
- ½ tsp. dried oregano
- ¼ tsp. cayenne pepper
- ¼ tsp. liquid smoke
- 2 Tbsp. olive oil
- 9 oz. package vegan chik'n cutlets (4 cutlets)
- 2 tsp. salt
- ½ tsp. black pepper

Rice:

- 1 cup brown rice
- 1 cup white quinoa, rinsed
- 4 cups water or vegetable broth

Directions

1. Place dried beans in a colander. Sort through them and remove any stones or debris. Rinse beans thoroughly while agitating them to release dirt.
2. Transfer beans to a 4-quart stock pot. Add cold water to a depth twice that of the beans. Cover and allow to soak overnight.
3. The next day, drain beans and return them to the stock pot. (If you forget to soak the beans overnight, you can accelerate the soaking process by rinsing the beans and placing them in 4-quart stockpot with cold water covering the beans by 2". Cover pot, bring to a boil, boil for two minutes, turn off the heat, and let stand for 2 hours. Drain, rinse, and return beans to pot. Add 1 hour to overall cooking time if using the quick-soak method.)
4. Add the broth, chorizo, onions, peppers, garlic, bay leaves, coriander, epazote, oregano, cayenne, and liquid smoke to the beans.
5. Stir gently, cover, and set pot over medium heat. Bring mixture to a boil, stirring occasionally.
6. Reduce heat to low. Simmer for 60–70 minutes until beans are cooked and tender. Stir occasionally.
7. About 45 minutes before serving, begin cooking the rice and quinoa mixture on the stovetop or in a rice cooker, according to the package instructions.
8. About 10 minutes before serving, heat a large frying pan over medium heat. Add the olive oil and swirl it around to cover the bottom of the pan.
9. Add the chik'n cutlets and pan-fry them until browned on the bottom (about 5 minutes). Flip and fry about 5 minutes more on the second side.
10. Remove cutlets from pan, slice each cutlet into 5 or 6 strips, and add all the strips + the salt and pepper to the bean mixture.
11. Stir gently to incorporate chik'n. Taste stew and adjust seasonings.
12. Serve bean mixture in individual bowls, ladled over portions of the cooked rice mixture.

CHILI

Makes 5 quarts; serves 12

This hearty vegetarian chili will satisfy even the carnivores at your table! I love everything about this recipe, including how it makes such a large batch. I make it either when I need to feed a crowd, or when I feel like chili for dinner and have time for the chopping and simmering. When I do the latter, I freeze $^2/_3$ of the batch for future dinnertimes when I don't have time for all that.

Ingredients

- 1 cup dried black beans (½ lb.)
- 1 cup dried pinto beans (½ lb.)
- water for soaking
- 1 cup medium pearl barley
- two 12 oz. bottles beer
- 3 cups vegetable broth (homemade, store-bought, or 3 cups water + 1 Tbsp. Better Than Bouillon vegetable or vegetarian chicken flavor)
- 1 bay leaf
- 2 medium white or yellow onions, diced
- 1 green bell pepper, diced (about 1 cup)
- 9 large cloves garlic, finely minced or pressed (3 Tbsp.)
- 1 jalapeño pepper with seeds, finely minced
- 1 Tbsp. chipotle peppers in adobo sauce, chopped to smithereens
- 4 oz. can diced mild green chile peppers
- 2 Tbsp. chili powder
- 1 ½ Tbsp. dried oregano
- 1 Tbsp. garlic powder
- 1 Tbsp. ground cumin
- four 28 oz. cans crushed tomatoes (or a #10 can)
- 32 oz. jar chunky salsa, medium-hot (about 4 cups)
- two 14 oz. cans dark red kidney beans, drained and rinsed
- 6 oz. can tomato paste
- 3 Tbsp. corn meal
- 1 Tbsp. brown sugar
- 1 Tbsp. apple cider vinegar
- ¼ tsp. jalapeño Tabasco

Directions

1. Place dried beans in a colander. Sort through them and remove any stones or debris. Rinse beans thoroughly while agitating them to release dirt.
2. Transfer beans to a 6-quart stock pot and add cold water to a depth twice that of the beans. Cover and allow to soak overnight.
3. The next day, drain beans and return them to the pot. (If you forget to soak the beans overnight, you can accelerate the soaking process by rinsing the beans and placing them in a 6-quart stockpot with cold water covering the beans by 2". Cover pot, bring to a boil, boil for two minutes, turn off the heat, and let stand for 2 hours. Drain, rinse, and return beans to pot. Add 1 hour to overall cooking time if using the quick-soak method.)
4. Add barley, beer, broth, and bay leaf to beans in pot.
5. Cover and place pot over medium-high heat. Bring to a boil.
6. Reduce heat to low. Allow mixture to simmer for 1 hour. Stir occasionally.
7. While beans are simmering, chop the vegetables and add the onions, peppers, garlic, and spices to the bean pot.
8. When the beans are completely cooked (check for doneness by tasting) add the remaining ingredients.
9. Stir in. Allow chili to simmer an additional 20 minutes.
10. Taste and adjust seasonings. Serve chili topped with grated cheese, a dollop of sour cream, and a scoop of diced avocado. Leftover chili freezes well.

Serving:

- 16 oz. bag grated cheddar cheese (4 cups)
- 16 oz. carton sour cream (2 cups)
- 3 ripe avocados, peeled and diced

CREAMY CHIK'N NOODLE SOUP

Makes 8 cups; serves 4

Vegetarian comfort food at its finest! Vegetarian chik'n cutlets step into the role of chicken most convincingly, and the homemade noodles in this soup are thick, rustic, and just the greatest thing ever. The noodles whip up quick, as they employ some of the simmering broth, which, believe you me, is a delicious idea.

Ingredients

Broth:
- 16 oz. package soft silken tofu, drained
- 5 cups water
- 3 Tbsp. Better Than Bouillon Vegetarian No Chicken Base

Soup:
- 2 Tbsp. vegetable oil
- 9.7 oz. package vegetarian chik'n cutlets (4 cutlets)
- 8 oz. package sliced mushrooms (any variety, about 3 cups)
- 2 Tbsp. snipped chives (fresh or dried)

Noodles:
- 1 cup all-purpose flour
- ½ cup whole wheat flour
- 1 tsp. salt
- ½ cup simmering broth from pot

Directions

1. **For Broth:** In container of blender or food processor, combine tofu, water, and bouillon.
2. Process on high until smooth. Set aside.
3. **For Soup:** Place a 3-quart stockpot over medium-high heat. Add oil.
4. When oil is hot, add chik'n cutlets and fry them for 4 minutes on each side.
5. Remove cutlets from pot and cut them into bite-sized pieces (about ¾" cubes).
6. Return chik'n to pot and add broth mixture, mushrooms, and chives. Reduce heat to medium-low and cover pot.
7. **For Noodles:** While soup is heating, in a medium mixing bowl, combine the flours and salt for the noodles.
8. When the soup is warmed and simmering, scoop out ½ cup of broth and add it to the flour mixture (be careful to scoop out just broth and not any mushrooms or chik'n cubes).
9. Stir the broth into the flour with a fork (dough will look rough). Knead dough for 1–2 minutes to fully distribute moisture throughout dough.
10. Cover bowl and let dough rest for 15 minutes.
11. After resting, knead the noodle dough gently and form it into a flat disc.
12. Transfer disc to a well-floured work surface. Roll dough out as thin as you can using a rolling pin (should roll to 12" in diameter and ⅛" thick).
13. Cut dough into strips ½" wide (a rolling pizza cutter works great for this). There is no need to be precise, as this is a rustic dish.
14. Rip strips into shorter lengths (3"–6") and drop them into the simmering soup, adding a new layer of noodles after the previous layer has sunk.
15. Cover pot and cook 10 minutes additional after last noodles are added.
16. Stir, taste, adjust seasonings, and serve. Leftover soup freezes well.

GUMBO
Makes 6 quarts; serves 12

Gumbo is a wonderfully complex, protein-rich stew that comes in many forms, as making it is open to individual interpretation and improvisation. Here, the traditional pork sausage and chicken thighs are replaced with vegetarian alternatives. The heat level of the veggie sausage you choose will determine the spiciness of the finished stew, so choose wisely! A dark roux is a key component of gumbo and usually quite time-consuming to produce. I have employed a shortcut here that involves toasting the flour before making the roux — ingenious!

Ingredients

Roux:
- ¾ cup all-purpose flour
- ½ cup vegetable oil

Gumbo:
- 3 Tbsp. vegetable oil, divided
- 9.7 oz. box vegetarian chik'n cutlets (4 cutlets)
- 1 large white or yellow onion, diced
- 1 green bell pepper, seeded and diced
- 6 ribs celery, diced (about 2 cups)
- 9 cloves garlic, finely minced or pressed (3 Tbsp.)
- 5 cups vegetable broth or water
- 12 oz. package veggie andouille sausage, chorizo, or kielbasa, sliced or crumbled
- 6 oz. package smoky tempeh or other vegetarian bacon, diced or crumbled
- 28 oz. can diced tomatoes
- two 4 oz. cans diced, mild green chile peppers
- 16 oz. bag frozen sliced okra, thawed
- 4 bay leaves
- 2 Tbsp. smoked paprika
- 1 tsp. dried oregano
- 1 tsp. salt
- ½ tsp. dried thyme
- ¼ tsp. dried sage
- ¼ tsp. black pepper
- 2 Tbsp. Worcestershire sauce

Rice:
- 3 cups brown rice
- 6 cups vegetable broth or water

Finishing:
- 2 lbs. raw shrimp, peeled and deveined
- 15 oz. can tomato sauce
- 1 bunch green onions, sliced
- ¼ cup minced fresh parsley or 2 Tbsp. dried parsley
- 2 Tbsp. gumbo file powder (ground sassafras leaves, essential for authentic flavor)
- 2 tsp. Tabasco-style hot pepper sauce

Directions

1. **For Roux:** Place an 8" skillet over medium-high heat. When the pan is hot, add the flour. Stir constantly with a whisk and cook for 5–10 minutes. Flour should be toasty, browned, and smell a little like popcorn.
2. Add oil to flour and whisk in. Continue to cook for 3 minutes, whisking constantly.
3. Remove roux from heat and set aside.
4. **For Gumbo:** Place an 8-quart stock pot over medium heat and add 2 Tbsp. oil.
5. When oil is hot, add chik'n cutlets. Cook for about 5 minutes on each side, until lightly browned.
6. Remove chik'n from pan and set aside.
7. Increase heat under pot to medium-high. Add 1 Tbsp. oil.
8. Add onion, pepper, celery, and garlic. Sauté vegetables, stirring almost constantly, until onion is translucent (about 10 minutes).
9. Add roux to vegetables. Stir until vegetables are coated.
10. Add broth. Stir until no lumps of roux remain. Cover and bring to a boil, stirring occasionally.
11. When mixture is boiling, add remaining gumbo ingredients. Stir. Reduce heat to low and cover.
12. Allow gumbo to simmer for 30 minutes. While gumbo is simmering, cook rice.
13. **For Rice:** On the stovetop or in a rice cooker, combine rice and broth. Cook according to package instructions.
14. **To Finish:** After gumbo has simmered, remove bay leaves (discard).
15. Add shrimp, tomato sauce, green onions, parsley, and file powder to gumbo. Stir in.
16. Cut the cooked chik'n cutlets into bite-sized pieces and add to gumbo pot. Cover. Allow gumbo to simmer for about 10 minutes until shrimp are pink, firm, and cooked through.
17. Taste gumbo and adjust seasonings. To serve, scoop rice into the bottom of individual bowls and ladle a generous portion of gumbo over top.

Gumbo is pictured on page 13

INDIAN STEW
Serves 8 to 12

This vegan stew takes time to make, but the time is both necessary (for the beans to cook and all the layers of flavor to develop) and worth it since this is a sophisticated, stupendous stew. Mercifully, this recipe makes a great big batch of the stuff, and the leftovers freeze well. So ... either make this for a party and impress the heck out of your guests, or make it for yourself and freeze little containers of it for you to enjoy on a moment's notice in the months to come.

Ingredients

Beans:
- 1 lb. black-eyed peas
- 5 cups vegetable broth (homemade, store-bought, or 5 cups water + 2 Tbsp. Better Than Bouillon vegetable)

Roasted Vegetables:
- 2 eggplants, cut into ¾" cubes (1 lb. each; about 8 cups total)
- 2 medium white or yellow onions, cut in 1" cubes (about 3 cups)
- 1 green bell pepper, cut in 1" cubes (about 1 ½ cups)
- 3 large carrots,** cut in ¼" thick slices (½ lb.; about 1 ½ cups)
- 6 large cloves garlic, minced (3 Tbsp.)
- ⅓ cup olive oil
- 1 tsp. salt

Stew:
- 4 oz. can diced, mild green chile peppers
- 6 oz. can tomato paste
- 4 tsp. ground coriander
- 2 ½ tsp. salt
- 2 tsp. garam masala (store-bought, or from recipe on page 151)
- 2 tsp. ground ginger
- 1 tsp. ground cumin
- 1 tsp. turmeric
- ½ tsp. cayenne pepper
- ½ tsp. ground black pepper
- ½ cup natural peanut butter (no sugar)
- ½ cup coconut milk (⅓ of a 14 oz. can)
- ½ cup chopped fresh cilantro

Quinoa:
- 3 cups pre-rinsed quinoa
- 6 cups broth or 6 cups water + 1 ½ tsp. salt

Directions

1. **For Beans:** Place dried beans in a colander. Sort through them and remove any stones or debris. Rinse beans thoroughly while agitating them to release dirt.
2. Transfer beans to a 6-quart stock pot and add cold water to a depth twice that of the beans. Cover and allow to soak overnight.
3. The next day, drain beans and return them to the pot. (If you forget to soak the beans overnight, you can accelerate the soaking process by rinsing the beans and placing them in a 6-quart stockpot with cold water covering the beans by 2". Cover pot, bring to a boil, boil for two minutes, turn off the heat, and let stand for 2 hours. Drain, rinse, and return beans to pot. Add 1 hour to overall cooking time if using the quick-soak method.)
4. Add broth to beans in pot, cover, place over medium-high heat and bring to a boil. Reduce heat to low and simmer for one hour, stirring occasionally. While beans are cooking, roast vegetables.
5. **For Vegetables:** Preheat oven to 400°.
6. In a large roasting pan (deep 9" x 13" pan), toss cut vegetables with olive oil and salt.
7. Roast vegetables, uncovered, for 1 hour, stirring once or twice during cooking.
8. Remove vegetables from oven and add to bean mixture.
9. **For Stew:** When beans are cooked, add chiles, tomato paste, and seasonings to the pot.
10. Cover, keep heat on low, and allow stew to simmer for 30 minutes more, stirring occasionally. While stew is simmering, cook quinoa according to package directions.
11. When quinoa is ready, add peanut butter, coconut milk, and cilantro to the stew and stir to combine. Remove from heat.
12. To serve, spoon quinoa into the bottom of individual bowls and ladle stew over top.

**NOTE: If making stew ahead of time and freezing it, omit the carrots and add them when re-heating.

LENTIL-BARLEY STEW

Makes 6 cups; serves 3-4

This hearty, vegan stew is a great choice to make for people who are hankering for a bowl of comfort. A classic, this stew is also a winner for kids who are picky eaters. Tip: If you are making this for someone who is squeamish about mushrooms, simply chop the mushrooms to smithereens, and I promise, they won't know they are in there.

Ingredients

- 2 Tbsp. olive oil
- 1 medium white or yellow onion, diced (about 1 ½ cups)
- 2 large carrots, diced ** (about 1 cup)
- 3 celery ribs, sliced (about 1 cup)
- 8 oz. package mushrooms, sliced (about 3 cups)
- 2 large cloves garlic, finely minced or pressed (2 tsp.)
- ¾ cup green, brown, or black lentils, rinsed
- ¼ cup pearl barley
- 1 tsp. dried thyme
- ½ tsp. dried basil
- ¼ tsp. dried oregano
- 4 cups vegetable broth (homemade, store-bought, or 4 cups water + 1 Tbsp. Better Than Bouillon vegetable or vegetarian chicken flavor)
- 2 Tbsp. soy sauce
- 1 Tbsp. dried parsley

Directions

1. Place a 3-quart saucepan over medium-high heat. Add oil.
2. When oil is hot, add onions, carrots, celery, mushrooms, and garlic.
3. Sauté vegetables until onions are translucent (about 5 minutes). Stir often.
4. Add lentils, barley, and herbs. Sauté one more minute.
5. Add broth, soy sauce, and parsley.
6. Reduce heat to low, cover, and simmer gently until lentils are tender (40-50 minutes). Stir occasionally.
7. Taste stew, adjust seasonings (salt may be needed) and serve.

**NOTE: Leftover stew freezes well. If making stew ahead and freezing it, omit the carrots and add them when reheating.

MIXED BEAN SOUP

Makes 12 cups; serves 6

This is a quintessential cold-winter's-day soup. Hearty and fortifying, it will warm your house and fill it with wonderful aromas as it simmers, and it will warm your tummy with goodness once it is done.

Ingredients

- 1 cup dried navy beans (½ lb.)
- 1 cup assorted other dried beans (½ lb.– no kidney beans)
- water for soaking
- 6 cups vegetable broth (homemade, store-bought, or 6 cups water + 2 Tbsp. Better Than Bouillon vegetable or vegetarian chicken flavor)
- 12 oz. package vegetarian chorizo, diced or crumbled
- 1 medium white or yellow onion, finely minced (about 1 ½ cups)
- 4 large cloves garlic, minced or pressed (4 tsp.)
- 2 carrots, thinly sliced or diced (about 1 cup)
- 1 bay leaf
- 2 tsp. dried thyme
- 1 tsp. ground celery seed
- ¼ tsp. ground cayenne pepper

Finishing:

- 28 oz. can diced tomatoes
- 5 oz. spinach, chopped (fresh or frozen)
- ½ tsp. salt

Directions

1. Place dried beans in a colander. Sort through them and remove any stones or debris. Rinse beans thoroughly while agitating them to release dirt.
2. Transfer beans to a 6-quart stockpot and add cold water to a depth twice that of the beans. Cover and allow to soak overnight.
3. The next day, drain beans and return them to the pot. (If you forget to soak the beans overnight, you can accelerate the soaking process by rinsing the beans and placing them in a 6-quart stockpot with cold water covering the beans by 2". Cover pot, bring to a boil, boil for 2 minutes, turn off the heat, and let stand for 2 hours. Drain, rinse, and return beans to pot. Add 1 hour to overall cooking time if using the quick-soak method.)
4. Add the broth, chorizo, onions, garlic, carrots, bay leaf, thyme, celery, and cayenne to the pot of beans. (Do not add tomatoes or salt at this point. They will prevent the beans from cooking properly.)
5. Cover pot and place over high heat. Bring to a boil.
6. Stir, reduce heat to low, cover, and allow to simmer for 60 minutes. Stir occasionally.
7. When beans are fully cooked (check for doneness by tasting) add the tomatoes, spinach, and salt. Stir well.
8. Taste soup, adjust seasonings, and serve. Leftover soup freezes well.

SEAFOOD CHOWDER

Makes 10 cups; serves 6

This is one of my all-time favorite dishes to make for company. People love it, and it is easy to prepare ahead of time and then finish at the last minute by tossing the seafood in as guests are arriving. You can mix and match seafood as you please, but at least some crab in the finished chowder is vital, as it adds a sweetness that balances everything out.

Ingredients

- 2 Tbsp. vegetable oil
- two 6 oz. packages smoky tempeh or other veggie bacon, diced
- 1 medium white or yellow onion, finely minced (about 1 ½ cups)
- 3 Tbsp. all-purpose flour
- 6 cups fish stock or 3 cups bottled clam juice + 3 cups water
- 1 large potato, washed and diced
- 16 oz. bag frozen sweet corn
- 3 lbs. seafood – any combination of shrimp (peeled, deveined), crab meat, clams (canned are fine), and scallops (bay are fine and less expensive)
- 1 cup heavy cream
- salt and pepper to taste

Directions

1. In a 4-quart stockpot over medium-high heat, add oil. Sauté tempeh until lightly browned and somewhat crispy.
2. Add onions to pot. Sauté until onions are translucent (2–3 minutes).
3. Add flour to make a roux. Stir flour into onions and bacon until no white spots of flour remain. Cook and stir for 1 minute more to eliminate raw flour flavor.
4. Add fish stock. Use whisk to incorporate broth and eliminate any lumps.
5. Cover. Bring broth to a boil, stirring occasionally. When mixture boils, stir constantly for 2 minutes until broth thickens slightly.
6. Add potato and corn, cover, and turn heat down to low. Allow chowder to simmer until potato is cooked (about 5 minutes). If making ahead, cook to this point and remove from heat. If making a day ahead, allow to cool and then chill, bringing it back to a simmer before proceeding with recipe.
7. Add seafood and cream to pot. Cover and bring back to a simmer. Cook until seafood is done (only takes 3–5 minutes). Scallops should be opaque, and shrimp should be pink and firm.
8. Taste. Add salt and pepper as needed. Remove from heat so the seafood doesn't overcook. Serve immediately.

SMOKED SALMON STEW

Makes 10 cups; serves 6-8

This stew is a bit unconventional but so, so good! Smoky, satisfying, and stupendous, serve it with fresh bread or crackers on the side and a nice tossed salad.

Ingredients

- 1 lb. dried white navy beans (2 cups)
- water for soaking
- 5 cups fish stock or 16 oz. bottled clam juice + water to make 5 cups
- 1 large white or yellow onion, diced (about 2 cups)
- 6 oz. package smoky tempeh or other veggie bacon, diced
- 15 oz. can golden hominy, drained and rinsed
- 4 oz. package smoked salmon (not nova style), skin removed, flesh crumbled into bite-sized pieces
- 2 hard-boiled eggs, peeled and diced (see page 3 for instructions, if needed)
- ½ tsp. salt

Directions

1. Place dried beans in a colander. Sort through them and remove any stones or debris. Rinse beans thoroughly while agitating them to release dirt.
2. Transfer beans to a 4-quart stockpot and add cold water to a depth twice that of the beans. Cover and allow to soak overnight.
3. The next day, drain beans and return them to the pot. (If you forget to soak the beans overnight, you can accelerate the soaking process by rinsing the beans and placing them in a 3-quart stockpot with cold water covering the beans by 2". Cover pot, bring to a boil, boil for two minutes, turn off the heat, and let stand for 2 hours. Drain, rinse, and return beans to pot. Add 1 hour to overall cooking time if using the quick-soak method.)
4. Add remaining ingredients except salt to the pot of beans.
5. Place pot over high heat and cover. Bring to a boil, stirring occasionally.
6. Reduce heat to low and allow stew to simmer for 60 minutes. Stir occasionally.
7. When beans are fully cooked (check for doneness by tasting) add the salt. Stir well.
8. Taste stew, adjust seasonings, and serve (add water if stew is too thick for your tastes). Leftover stew freezes well.

SPICY LENTIL SOUP

Makes 3 quarts; serves 6-8

You can certainly ramp up the heat intensity of this soup by adding more hot peppers to the veggie mix, but I have found that the balance of flavors is best with a medium heat in the finished soup. Also, there are really good vegan chorizos out there, which makes a vegan version of this soup possible.

Ingredients

- 2 Tbsp. olive oil
- 1 large white or yellow onion, diced (about 2 cups)
- 1 red bell pepper, diced (about 1 ½ cups)
- 1 jalapeño pepper, seeded and finely minced
- 2 large cloves garlic, minced or smashed (2 tsp.)
- 2 tsp. ground cumin
- 8 cups vegetable broth (homemade, store-bought, or 8 cups water + 3 Tbsp. Better Than Bouillon vegetable or vegetarian chicken flavor)
- 2 cups green, brown, or black lentils, rinsed (1 lb.)
- 12 oz. veggie chorizo, diced or crumbled
- 28 oz. can diced tomatoes
- 1 Tbsp. cider vinegar
- 1 tsp. salt
- ¼ tsp. ground black pepper

Directions

1. In 4-quart stock pot, heat oil over medium-high heat. Sauté onions, peppers, garlic, and cumin until onions are translucent and soft.
2. Add broth, lentils, and chorizo. Cover and bring to a boil.
3. Reduce heat to low and simmer for 20–40 minutes depending on the variety of lentils used.
4. When lentils are done (check by tasting), add remaining ingredients and heat through. Taste, adjust seasonings and serve. Leftover soup freezes well.

SPLIT PEA SOUP

Makes 8 cups; serves 4-6

I like my split pea soup to be flavorful and comforting, so that's what this is. Blessed with wonderful tastes and textures, I have served this humble soup to guests who raved.

Ingredients

- 2 Tbsp. olive or vegetable oil
- 6 oz. package smoky tempeh or other veggie bacon, diced
- 1 medium yellow or white onion, diced (about 1 ½ cups)
- 8 oz. package sliced mushrooms (about 3 cups)
- 2 big carrots, diced (1 cup)
- 4 large cloves garlic, minced or pressed (4 tsp.)
- 1 tsp. ground celery seed
- 1 tsp. dried thyme
- ½ tsp. salt
- 8 cups vegetable broth (homemade, store-bought, or 8 cups water + 3 Tbsp. Better Than Bouillon vegetable or vegetarian chicken flavor)
- 2 cups dried split peas (1 lb.)
- ¼ cup pearl barley
- ¼ cup buckwheat (kasha)
- 1 cup grated fresh Parmesan or Asiago cheese
- 1 Tbsp. balsamic vinegar

Directions

1. In a 4-quart stock pot over medium-high heat, add oil and tempeh. Sauté until tempeh is lightly browned and somewhat crispy.
2. Add onions, mushrooms, carrots, and garlic to pot. Sauté until onions are translucent.
3. Add celery seed, thyme, and salt. Stir until spices are fragrant (less than a minute).
4. Add broth, split peas, barley, and buckwheat to pot. Stir. Cover and bring to a boil.
5. Reduce heat to low. Allow soup to simmer for 30 minutes, until peas and barley are tender.
6. Add cheese and vinegar to pot. Stir until cheese is melted. Serve hot.

TARASCAN INDIAN SOUP

Makes 6 cups; serves 3-4

Tarascan Indians hail from southwestern Mexico, and this soup features ingredients and spices common to that region. The heat from the peppers is mild, but the flavor of the finished soup is robust and satisfying. Best of all, if you use jarred peppers, it throws together in no time.

Ingredients

Soup:

- 16 oz. jar roasted red bell peppers, with liquid (or 3 red bell peppers, roasted, peeled, and seeded + ½ cup water)
- 4 oz. can diced, mild green chile peppers (or 2 ancho chile peppers, roasted and peeled)
- 2 cups vegetable broth (homemade, store-bought, or 2 cups water + 2 tsp. Better Than Bouillon vegetable or vegetarian chicken flavor)
- 2 Tbsp. vegetable or olive oil
- 2 vegetarian chik'n cutlets (½ of a 9 oz. box)
- 1 medium yellow or white onion, finely minced (about 1 ½ cups)
- 3 large cloves garlic, finely minced or pressed (1 Tbsp.)
- two 15 oz. cans hominy or pozole (corn), drained and rinsed
- 1 tsp. lime juice
- 1 tsp. dried epazote (Mexican oregano) or dried oregano
- ½ tsp. salt
- ¼ tsp. ground black pepper

Toppings:

- 1 ½ cups shredded cheddar cheese (6 oz.)
- 1 cup crushed tortilla chips
- ½ cup sour cream

Directions

1. In a blender or food processor, dump bell peppers, chile peppers, and broth. Process on high until smooth. Set aside.
2. Heat oil in 3-quart stockpot over medium heat. Add chik'n cutlets and fry for 4 minutes on each side.
3. Remove cutlets from pan and cut into ¼" thick slices.
4. Return stockpot to heat. Sauté onion and garlic for 3 minutes, stirring almost constantly.
5. Add pureed pepper mixture, sliced chik'n cutlets, hominy, lime juice, epazote, salt, and pepper. Cover and heat to boiling.
6. Remove from heat and serve in individual bowls with a handful of grated cheese, sprinkling of crushed tortilla chips, and dollop of sour cream on top. Leftover soup freezes well.

WHITE BEAN SOUP

Makes 12 cups, serves 6-8

My husband had the idea for this soup and made an early version of it. Wonderfully warming and peppery, it is just the thing for a cold winter day! The silken tofu adds a creaminess while maintaining this soup's vegan status.

Ingredients

- 1 lb. white navy beans (2 cups)
- water for soaking
- 6 cups vegetable broth (homemade, store-bought, or 6 cups water + 2 Tbsp. Better Than Bouillon vegetable or vegetarian chicken flavor)
- ½ cup medium pearl barley
- 4 cups diced white or yellow onions (2 large onions)
- 2 tsp. finely minced or pressed garlic (2 large cloves)
- 5 oz. chopped spinach (fresh or frozen), optional
- 1 bay leaf
- 1 tsp. dried thyme
- 1 tsp. ground rosemary
- 6 shakes liquid smoke

Finishing:

- 16 oz. package soft silken tofu, drained
- 1 cup vegetable broth or water
- 2 tsp. salt
- 1 ½ tsp. ground black pepper

Directions

1. Place dried beans in a colander. Sort through them and remove any stones or debris. Rinse beans thoroughly while agitating them to release dirt.
2. Transfer beans to a 3-quart stock pot. Add cold water to a depth twice that of the beans. Cover and allow to soak overnight.
3. The next day, drain beans and return them to the stock pot. (If you forget to soak the beans overnight, you can accelerate the soaking process by rinsing the beans and placing them in a 3-quart stockpot with cold water covering the beans by 2". Cover pot, bring to a boil, boil for two minutes, turn off the heat, and let stand for 2 hours. Drain, rinse, and return beans to pot. Add 1 hour to overall cooking time if using the quick-soak method.)
4. Add broth, barley, onions, garlic, spinach, bay leaf, thyme, rosemary, and smoke to beans in pot.
5. Cover pot and place over high heat. Bring to a boil, stirring occasionally.
6. Reduce heat to low, stir, cover, and allow soup to simmer for 60 minutes.
7. When beans are cooked and tender (check by tasting), place tofu, water, salt, and pepper in the container of a blender or food processor fitted with a blade.
8. Process tofu on low speed until mixture is smooth.
9. Add tofu mixture to beans in pot. Stir well.
10. Taste soup, adjust seasonings, and serve. Leftover soup freezes well.

Tabbouleh Salad with Shrimp, recipe on page 31

MAIN DISH SALADS

No matter where you live, when hot weather strikes, you want to be eating lighter, chillier food. It is not news to anyone that lasagna is just not a summer picnic thing. Certainly, on a hot day, grabbing leftovers and eating them cold from the fridge is one way to go, but so is a chilled salad. And here is a whole chapter of them. The recipes range from crisp lettuces to whole grains to pastas and back again, with a chilly salad for practically every appetite.

CRAB COBB SALAD

Serves 2

I love this salad. I love everything about this salad. The flavors are just spectacular together, and guests I have served this salad to just rave and rave about it.

Ingredients

Salad:

- 8 cups chopped romaine lettuce (12 oz. bag romaine hearts = 12 cups chopped lettuce)
- 6 oz. pouch lump crab meat, or two 6 oz. cans lump crab meat, drained
- 4 oz. smoky tempeh, or other vegetarian bacon, pan-fried and crumbled
- 1 avocado, pitted, peeled, and sliced or diced

Dressing:

- ½ cup bleu cheese salad dressing (store-bought or homemade from recipe on page 153)

Directions

1. Divide lettuce on two dinner plates.
2. Top lettuce with crab meat, bacon, and avocado, layered in that order. Divide toppings evenly between the two salads and use everything up.
3. Drop dollops of blue cheese dressing over all. Serve immediately.

GREEK TORTELLINI PASTA SALAD

Makes 8 cups; serves 4–6

This salad is a favorite of my carnivorous son. Back when we were omnivores, I made this salad with grilled, boneless, skinless, chicken breasts. But now that we are pescatarians, I make it with vegetarian chik'n cutlets, and I swear no one notices the difference.

Ingredients

Chik'n:

- 2 Tbsp. olive or vegetable oil
- 9.7 oz. package vegetarian chik'n cutlets (4 cutlets)

Salad:

- 12 oz. package dried, shelf-stable cheese tortellini or two 12 oz. packages fresh or frozen cheese tortellini (5 cups tortellini when cooked)
- 14 oz. can artichoke hearts, drained and cut top-to-bottom in thin wedges
- 6 oz. can sliced black olives or small olives left whole, drained
- 2 cups halved cherry tomatoes (1 pint) or diced beefsteak tomato
- ½ cup diced or thinly sliced red onion or green onions (2–3 onions)
- 4 oz. crumbled feta cheese (1 cup)

Dressing:

- 1 ¼ cups Greek vinaigrette (store-bought or homemade from recipe on page 155)

Directions

1. **For Chik'n:** Heat oil in small frying pan over medium heat.
2. Add chik'n cutlets and fry until browned on the bottom (about 5 minutes). Flip, then fry for 5 minutes more.
3. Remove cutlets from pan and set aside to cool.
4. When cooled, cut chik'n into ¼" thick slices or ½" cubes.
5. **For Salad:** While chik'n is cooking and cooling, cook tortellini just until al dente, according to package instructions. Drain pasta.
6. Rinse pasta briefly in cold water to arrest cooking process. Transfer cooked tortellini to a large mixing bowl.
7. Add remaining salad ingredients to bowl. Add cooled chik'n.
8. Pour dressing over ingredients. Mix very gently with a rubber spatula, so you don't break up the tortellini.
9. Cover and chill salad. Serve chilled.

SMOKED SALMON AND GOAT CHEESE SALAD

Serves 2

I keep a batch of homemade Raspberry Vinaigrette on hand, so when the need for "dinner in a flash" arises, I am prepared. With vinaigrette on hand, this salad comes together in about 5 minutes.

Ingredients

Salad:

- 8 cups roughly chopped lettuce (8 oz.)
- ½ cup thinly sliced red onion
- 4 oz. package smoked salmon
- 4 Tbsp. chopped walnuts
- 2 oz. goat cheese, crumbled (¼ cup)

Dressing:

- ½ cup raspberry vinaigrette (store-bought or homemade from recipe on page 156)

Directions

1. Divide lettuce onto two dinner plates.
2. Top lettuce with onions, salmon, walnuts, and cheese, dividing toppings evenly between the two salads.
3. Drizzle salads with raspberry vinaigrette and serve.

TABBOULEH SALAD WITH SHRIMP

Makes 12 cups; serves 6-8

Many people make tabbouleh like a parsley salad, with a bit of bulgur wheat thrown in for good measure. I, however, prefer my tabbouleh made in the reverse — as a grain salad, with a bit of parsley thrown in for flavor and micronutrients. This salad takes all of that a step further, with the inclusion of pasta, shrimp, and garbanzo beans, elevating a humble tabbouleh into a complete meal.

Ingredients

Bulgur Wheat:
- 1 cup bulgur wheat
- 2 cups boiling water

Pasta:
- ½ cup Mediterranean pearl couscous or orzo pasta

Salad:
- 1 lb. peeled, de-veined, cooked shrimp (for a vegan salad, substitute 4 pan-fried, diced vegan chik'n filets)
- 15 oz. can garbanzo beans (chick peas), drained
- 2 cups diced cucumber (6"–8" cucumber)
- 2 cups halved cherry tomatoes (1 pint), or 1 large beefsteak tomato, diced
- 1 cup thinly sliced red onion or green onions (about 1 grocery store bunch)
- 1 cup minced fresh parsley (about 1 grocery store bunch)
- ¼ cup minced fresh mint or cilantro
- 2 tsp. salt
- ½ tsp. ground black pepper
- ¾ cup olive oil
- ¾ cup fresh lemon juice (2–3 lemons)

Directions

1. **For Bulgur Wheat:** Place the bulgur wheat and boiling water in a small mixing bowl. Cover and let stand for one hour.
2. When all the water has been absorbed and the bulgur wheat is tender, transfer it to a large mixing bowl. Cover and chill.
3. **For Pasta:** Cook pasta until al dente according to package instructions. Drain and add to bulgur wheat in bowl.
4. **For Salad:** Add the remaining salad ingredients to the bowl of bulgur wheat and couscous.
5. Stir gently to combine. Cover and refrigerate until serving time. Best if allowed to chill for at least 2 hours before serving for liquids to absorb and flavors to meld. Flavor is even better if salad is made a day ahead of serving.

THAI COLD NOODLE SALAD

Serves 6-8

A lot of Thai food is not so good for a diabetic or a dieter because it contains so much sugar. If you make your own vinaigrette from my recipe on page 157, this salad is quite the exception, as it has all the wonderful flavor from a Thai ginger-peanut sauce but only 1 tsp. sugar in the whole six to eight servings. Unusual and unforgettable, this salad is a real winner.

Ingredients

Salad:

- 1 lb. tuna steaks
- Salt and pepper
- 1 Tbsp. vegetable oil
- 16 oz. rice noodles (brown or white rice)
- 16 oz. frozen sugar snap peas or snow pea pods, thawed
- 1 ½ cups thinly sliced radishes (1 grocery store bunch)

Dressing:

- 2 cups Thai Vinaigrette from recipe on page 157, or store-bought Thai peanut sauce or pad Thai sauce

Directions

1. Heat an 8" cast iron frying pan over medium-high heat for 5-10 minutes.
2. Lightly season tuna steaks with salt and pepper.
3. When frying pan is good and hot, add oil and swirl it around to coat the bottom of the pan.
4. Return pan to burner and add tuna steaks.
5. Flash-fry steaks for exactly 45 seconds on each side and remove immediately from pan. Set aside to cool.
6. While pan is heating for the tuna steaks, heat water for the pasta. Half-fill a 4-quart stock pot with water, add 2 tsp. salt, cover, and place over high heat.
7. When pasta water comes to a boil, break dried pasta noodles in half and cook according to package instructions.
8. Drain noodles, rinse in cold water, and transfer to a large mixing bowl.
9. Immediately add the vinaigrette and toss very gently to combine. If, for some reason, you cannot add the vinaigrette right away, let the noodles soak in cold water until you are ready, in order to keep the noodles from sticking together in a giant lump.
10. Cut cooled tuna steaks into thin slices (¼" thick) and add to cooked pasta along with the pea pods and radishes.
11. Toss very gently (hands work best for this) until all ingredients are well mixed and evenly coated in vinaigrette. Cover and refrigerate until serving time. Serve chilled.

Nut Burger, recipe on page 41

BURGERS AND SANDWICHES

If my two sons were to ever open a restaurant, it would be a sandwich shop, as they are great cooks, adventurous eaters, AND big-time sandwich connoisseurs. Between the two of them, they can make anything into a sandwich. They might come to blows in the kitchen, but their collaborations would be inventive and incredible.

I hope I have inspired them, but where sandwiches are concerned, it pains me greatly to admit that my honest-to-God favorite sandwich is my Lonely Girl Special — a fried egg and cheese sandwich on toast (organic egg, fancy cheese, homemade bread, but still….). It has that name because it is my dinner of choice when my husband is out-of-town. When on my own, I become embarrassingly melodramatic over eating dinner alone, and fix myself the saddest, most comforting thing I can think of: that sandwich. Yes, every night that he's gone. I thought it was just me that did this, but no. My sister's Lonely Girl Special is a baloney sandwich, a former neighbor's is ice cream and cottage cheese, a friend's is a baked potato bar for one (baked potato with every leftover in the fridge on top).

I am not going to go so far as to claim that a good sandwich can cure loneliness, but I will assert that a great sandwich can make you feel that there is good in the world, and can give you the strength to soldier on.

CHIK'N CAESAR WRAP

Makes 4 wraps

I swear on all that is holy that no one who eats these will ever guess that they are vegetarian! Full-flavored and incredibly satisfying, once you try them, you will want one of these packed in your lunchbox, like, every day.

Ingredients

Eggs:
- 4 eggs

Chik'N:
- 3 Tbsp. olive or vegetable oil
- 9.7 oz. box vegetarian chik'n cutlets, thawed (4 cutlets)

Filling:
- 4 cups torn or chopped romaine lettuce leaves (4 oz.)
- ⅓ cup Caesar salad dressing (store-bought or homemade from recipe on page 154)
- ¼ cup grated Parmesan cheese

Serving:
- four 8" whole-grain tortillas or flatbread wraps

Directions

1. **For Eggs:** Hard boil the eggs (directions on page 3, if needed), and set to cool in cold water. When eggs are cool, peel.
2. **For Chik'n:** While eggs are cooling, cook chik'n. In a large frying pan over medium heat, place oil.
3. When oil is hot, add chik'n cutlets to pan. Fry cutlets until they are browned on the bottom (about 5 minutes).
4. Flip cutlets over and fry on the other side (about 5 minutes).
5. Transfer cooked cutlets to a cutting board. Cut each cutlet crosswise into ¼" thick strips.
6. **To Assemble:** Lay the tortillas out on a work surface. Slice one hard-boiled egg and place the slices in a row down the center of one tortilla. Repeat process with other eggs and tortillas.
7. In a small mixing bowl, toss the lettuce with the Caesar dressing until all the lettuce is coated in dressing.
8. Top each tortilla with a handful of lettuce, arranging it over top of the sliced eggs. Divide the lettuce evenly between the tortillas, and use it all up.
9. Top the lettuce with sliced chik'n, using one cutlet for each wrap.
10. Top everything with Parmesan cheese, using 1 Tbsp. for each wrap.
11. Fold up the bottom edge of the tortilla to keep the filling from falling out, and fold the two sides around the filling.

CRAB WRAP

Makes 8 burrito-sized wraps

I tried (really I did) to create a tasty crab burrito, but it just never worked. Flavors competed for dominance, and no matter the combination of ingredients, the results were kind of terrible. However ... the idea for this Crab Wrap came out of all that mess, and these suckers are fantastic. The flavors and textures are balanced and the crab is star of the show.

Ingredients

Crab:

- 8 oz. lump crab meat
- 8 oz. imitation crab meat, diced or thinly sliced
- 8 oz. package queso blanco cheese, crumbled

Coleslaw:

- 16 oz. package coleslaw mix or 5 cups shredded cabbage and carrots
- 1 cup paper-thin slices of red onion
- ¼ cup mayonnaise
- 2 Tbsp. lime juice
- 2 tsp. Tabasco-style hot pepper sauce
- 1 tsp. salt

Guacamole:

- 6 avocados, peeled and pitted
- 1 Tbsp. lime juice
- 2 tsp. minced garlic (2 cloves), smashed to a paste with ½ tsp. salt
- 1 ½ tsp. dried dill weed
- ½ tsp. ground cumin

Wrap:

- 8 burrito-sized tortillas, warmed

Directions

1. **For Crab:** In a medium mixing bowl, combine ingredients for crab mixture. Stir well. Set aside.
2. **For Coleslaw:** In a large mixing bowl, combine ingredients for the coleslaw. Stir until the shredded vegetables are evenly coated in the other ingredients.
3. **For Guacamole:** In a medium mixing bowl, smash the avocados with a potato masher or fork, leaving the mixture slightly chunky.
4. Add remaining ingredients for guacamole and mix vigorously.
5. **To Assemble:** Warm tortillas in the microwave, or wrap and heat them in the oven.
6. Lay tortillas out, and top each with ⅛ of the crab mixture (about ½ cup) in a rectangle down the middle of the tortilla, then ⅛ of the coleslaw mixture on top (about ½ cup), and ⅛ of the guacamole over all (about ¼ cup).
7. Fold tortilla around filling burrito-style (front side over, two ends tucked in, roll to enclose everything). Slice across the middle (this makes it easier to handle) and eat.

CRAM CAKES

Makes 8 burger-sized patties

Well, what would you call a seafood burger that's crammed full of a combination of lump crab meat and chopped clams? A Cram Cake, of course! These require lump crab meat for flavor and texture, so if all you have on hand is imitation crab or cans of snow crab, please make something else for dinner.

Ingredients

Burger Mix:

- 16 oz. package chopped fresh clams + ¼ cup of their juice (or 10 oz. package frozen cooked clams + ¼ cup clam juice or three 5 oz. cans chopped clams + ¼ cup of their juice)
- 8 oz. package lump crab meat (or two 6 oz. cans lump crab meat, drained)
- 3 large eggs
- ¼ cup red bell pepper, finely minced (¼ of a pepper)
- 1 cup dried bread or cracker crumbs
- 4 tsp. onion powder (bust up any lumps)
- 2 tsp. dried sage
- 1 tsp. Old Bay Seasoning
- ¼ tsp. ground black pepper

Frying:

- 2 Tbsp. olive or vegetable oil

Serving:

- ¼ cup Sriracha mayonnaise (store-bought or homemade: ¼ cup mayonnaise + ¾ tsp. Sriracha hot chili sauce)
- 8 whole-grain buns (optional)

Directions

1. Inspect clams and cut any large pieces into a small dice.
2. In a medium mixing bowl, combine all ingredients for burgers and mix thoroughly.
3. Heat a large frying pan or griddle over medium heat.
4. When pan is hot, add oil and swirl to coat bottom of pan.
5. Using ½ cup measure as a scoop, drop scoopfuls of burger mix into the pan, pressing each into a patty ½" thick and 4" wide.
6. Cook patties for 3 – 5 minutes on each side (burger will be firm to the touch when done).
7. Serve Cram Cakes on buns or naked, with Sriracha mayonnaise on top.

Note: Cram Cakes may be made ahead and frozen before frying. Wrap each patty individually in plastic wrap, then place all of them in a zip-top freezer bag. Cram Cakes will keep for several months in the freezer. Thaw before frying.

FRIED FISH SANDWICH

Makes 6 – 8 sandwiches

I struggled for years to figure out a way to make crispy fried fish that would stay crispy when made into a sandwich. Here it is. This method is nothing short of brilliant, and you are welcome.

Ingredients

Oil:
- 8 cups vegetable oil for deep frying (64 oz.)

Fish:
- 2 lb. cod, flounder, or haddock filets

Batter:
- 2 large eggs
- 1 cup buttermilk
- ½ cup all-purpose flour
- ½ cup cornmeal
- 1 Tbsp. Old Bay Seasoning
- ½ tsp. salt
- ¼ tsp. ground black pepper

Breading:
- 2 ½ cups panko-style bread crumbs

Serving:
- 6 – 8 toasted wholegrain buns, English muffins, or tortillas for wraps
- ¾ cup tartar sauce (store-bought or homemade from recipe on page 163)
- lettuce leaves (optional)

Directions

1. **For Frying:** In a stockpot, deep frying pan, electric fryer, or wok, heat oil to 350° (a deep-fry thermometer is invaluable). Oil should be at least 3" deep. Line a baking sheet with several layers of paper towels or newspaper, lay a cooling rack upside down on top of paper, and set aside.
2. Cut fish filets into bun-sized pieces. Pat fish dry.
3. **For Batter:** In a small mixing bowl, combine eggs and buttermilk. Whisk together.
4. Add remaining batter ingredients and blend in. Set aside.
5. **For Breading:** Dump bread crumbs in a broad, shallow bowl or pie plate.
6. When oil is up to temperature, begin frying fish. Working with a few pieces of fish at a time, dip fish in batter, allow excess batter to drip off, and dredge in bread crumbs to coat.
7. Drop fish into hot oil.
8. Repeat dipping and coating process with remaining fish pieces, being careful to not over-crowd the oil (cook fish in batches, as needed).
9. Fry fish pieces for about 6 minutes, flipping them over in the middle of the cooking time.
10. Remove fried fish from oil with tongs or a kitchen spider and lay on prepared tray to drain. If frying fish in batches, keep first batches warm in a 200° oven while frying the rest.
11. Serve fried fish on buns, English muffins, or in tortillas, topped with tartar sauce and lettuce.

FALAFEL

Serves 8

I will admit, I love both the convenience and the flavor of boxed falafel mix. Despite that, I don't love how low its protein content is, as the boxed stuff lacks good complementary plant proteins. So ... my way of making falafel corrects for that nutritionally, is definitely a step above taste-wise, and is only slightly more work than the box — seriously, give it a try! Also, this falafel mixture (before frying) freezes extremely well. Make a double-batch, freeze the extra mix in covered containers, and your next falafel night will be easy-peasy!

Ingredients

Falafel:

- 1 lb. dried chickpeas (2 cups) – do not substitute canned in this recipe
- water for soaking
- 1 cup pecans or walnuts
- 3 cups roughly chopped white or yellow onion (2 medium onions)
- 6 large cloves garlic, peeled (2 Tbsp.)
- ¼ cup roughly chopped fresh parsley or 2 Tbsp. dried parsley
- 2 tsp. lemon juice
- 1 Tbsp. salt
- 1 Tbsp. ground coriander
- 1 tsp. ground cumin
- 1 tsp. ground turmeric
- ½ tsp. ground cardamom
- ¼ tsp. ground black pepper
- ¼ tsp. cayenne pepper

Frying:

- ½ cup olive or vegetable oil

Serving:

- 8 pita breads
- 1 cup tahini (store-bought), tzatziki sauce (store-bought or from recipe on page 163), or toum (store-bought or from recipe on page 163)
- 3 beefsteak tomatoes, diced or sliced, or 2 pints (4 cups) cherry tomatoes, cut in halves
- 1 cup thinly sliced red onion
- lettuce leaves
- 8 oz. crumbled feta cheese

Directions

1. Place dried chickpeas in a colander. Sort through them and remove any stones or debris. Rinse chickpeas thoroughly while agitating them to release dirt.
2. Transfer chickpeas to a large mixing bowl and add cold water to a depth twice that of the beans. Allow to soak for 8 hours or overnight.
3. After soaking, drain chickpeas.
4. In bowl of food processor fitted with a steel blade, or into a meat grinder, place soaked chickpeas, nuts, onion, garlic, parsley, and lemon juice. Run everything through the meat grinder once or process in the food processor until very finely chopped, but stop before mixture becomes a paste. The proper texture will be between couscous and peanut butter.
5. Transfer mixture back into the large mixing bowl. Add remaining ingredients for falafel and stir well.
6. Cover bowl and let mixture rest for 15 minutes (this allows the starch to develop so the finished balls or patties hold together).
7. In a large frying pan over medium heat, place 1 Tbsp. of oil. Swirl pan to coat bottom in oil.
8. Form dough into balls that are slightly smaller than a golf ball (1 ½ Tbsp. each). Pan-fry balls in batches, placing balls in frying pan in a single layer, being careful to not over-crowd pan. Immediately press lightly on balls to flatten them slightly.
9. Fry falafel for 3 – 5 minutes on first side, flip over, and fry for 3 – 5 minutes on second side.
10. Remove falafel from pan. Repeat frying process with remaining falafel mix, adding 1 Tbsp. oil to pan before each batch.
11. Serve falafel hot or at room temperature. To eat, assemble falafel patties into a sandwich by stuffing them inside pocket pita halves, or by laying them open-face style on top of pita bread. Add tomatoes, onions, lettuce, and feta, and drizzle with your choice of tahini, tzatziki, or toum.

LENTIL BURGERS

Makes 6 large burgers

I was given a version of this recipe by my sister many years ago, when she was on a macrobiotic kick. I have revised and tweaked that recipe many times over the years, improving the flavor, texture, and protein content. My new-and-improved version is probably not as macrobiotic, but definitely tastier!

Ingredients

Burger Mix:

- ½ cup green, brown, or black lentils
- ¼ cup brown rice
- ¼ cup pearl barley
- 2 cups vegetable broth or water
- 1 large egg
- ½ cup bread or cracker crumbs
- ¼ cup wheat germ (optional)
- ½ cup finely minced white or yellow onion
- ¼ tsp. ground celery seed
- ¼ tsp. marjoram (or ¼ tsp. thyme + ¼ tsp. turmeric)
- ¼ tsp. salt
- ¼ tsp. black pepper

Breading and Frying:

- ⅓ cup corn meal, bread crumbs, or cracker crumbs
- 3 Tbsp. vegetable or olive oil for frying

Serving:

- 6 whole grain hamburg buns or English muffins, toasted
- Your choice of burger toppings and condiments (ketchup, mustard, mayo, sliced tomato, sliced red onion, sliced cheese, lettuce)

Directions

1. In a 2-quart saucepan over medium-high heat, combine lentils, rice, barley, and broth. Cover and bring mixture to a boil.
2. Stir, reduce heat to low (2 on a scale of 1 to 10), and allow mixture to simmer (covered) until grains are tender (30 – 45 minutes). Remove from heat.
3. Mash grains with a fork or potato masher until they begin to bind. Add remaining burger ingredients. Mix thoroughly.
4. Divide mixture into 6 portions (about ½ cup each) and shape each into a round, flat patty.
5. Place corn meal in a shallow bowl or on a small plate and dip each patty in corn meal to coat both sides.
6. Heat oil in a large frying pan over medium heat.
7. Add burgers and cook until browned on bottom (3 – 5 minutes). Flip and cook until browned on the second side.
8. Serve Lentil Burgers on buns with your choice of toppings and condiments.

Note: Lentil Burgers may be made ahead and frozen before frying. Wrap each burger individually in plastic wrap, then place them in a zip-top freezer bag. Lentil Burgers will keep for several months in the freezer. Thaw before frying.

NUT BURGERS

Makes 7 burgers

It took me quite a few tries to create a veggie nut burger with good protein content, pleasing textures, and delicious flavor. I am glad I kept at it, as these burgers are fantastic, and definitely all three of those things. To make these burgers vegan, replace the eggs in the recipe with ½ cup of the liquid drained off a can of chickpeas (it's amazing stuff!).

Ingredients

Roasted mushrooms:

- 16 oz. white mushrooms, sliced (6 cups)
- 1 Tbsp. olive or vegetable oil
- ¼ tsp. salt

Roasted nuts:

- ¾ cup finely chopped walnuts (largest pieces the size of sunflower seeds)
- ½ cup finely chopped almonds (largest pieces the size of sunflower seeds)
- ¼ cup sunflower seeds

Burger mix:

- 15 oz. can black beans, drained and rinsed
- 8 oz. regular or smoky tempeh
- 2 Tbsp. finely minced or pressed garlic (6 large cloves)
- 2 eggs (for vegan burgers, use ½ cup chickpea "juice")
- ¼ cup soy or quinoa flour
- ¼ tsp. ground black pepper
- 2 tsp. soy sauce
- 1 tsp. peanut oil

Frying:

- 2 Tbsp. olive or vegetable oil

Serving:

- 7 whole grain hamburg buns or English muffins, toasted
- your choice of burger toppings and condiments (ketchup, mustard, mayo, sliced tomato, sliced red onion, sliced cheese, lettuce)

Directions

1. **For Mushrooms:** Preheat oven to 400°.
2. In a medium mixing bowl, toss mushrooms with oil and salt. Transfer mushrooms to a greased baking sheet and spread to an even layer.
3. Roast mushrooms for 20 minutes, until mushrooms are browned and fairly dry.
4. Remove mushrooms from oven and finely chop.
5. **For Nuts:** Place chopped nuts and seeds in a dry skillet over medium heat.
6. Cook, stirring constantly, until nuts are lightly toasted and fragrant (5 – 7 minutes).
7. **For Burgers:** In medium mixing bowl, mash beans with a fork.
8. Add chopped, roasted mushrooms, roasted nuts, and remaining ingredients for burgers.
9. Mix until thoroughly combined.
10. Using a ½ cup measure as a scoop, portion the burger mixture into 7 patties. Press each portion into a round patty that is about 3 ½" in diameter and ½" thick. Nut Burgers don't shrink or expand during cooking, so they can also be made to fit whatever buns you will be serving them on.
11. **To Cook:** Heat a large frying pan over medium heat and add the 2 Tbsp. oil.
12. When the oil is hot, add the burgers to the pan and fry for 3 – 4 minutes on each side. Burgers should be lightly browned and firm when done.
13. Serve on toasted whole grain buns with the toppings and condiments of your choice.

Note: Nut Burgers may be made ahead and frozen before frying. Wrap each burger individually in plastic wrap, then place them in a zip-top freezer bag. Nut Burgers will keep for several months in the freezer. Thaw before frying.

Nut Burger is pictured on page 33

SALMON PATTIES

Makes 3 patties

These are fast, easy, and oh-so-good! If you don't want big burgers, the salmon mix can be fried up in small croquettes. Serve them as an appetizer or finger food with Ranch dressing for dipping, or stuff the little buggers into pitas.

Ingredients

Patties:

- 7.1 oz. pouch boneless, skinless pink salmon or two 5 oz. cans boneless, skinless pink salmon drained
- ¼ cup bread or cracker crumbs
- 1 large egg
- 1 Tbsp. dried chives
- 2 tsp. brown mustard
- 1 tsp. onion powder
- 1 tsp. dried dill weed
- 1 tsp. Sriracha chili pepper hot sauce or 1 tsp. prepared horseradish

Frying:

- 3 Tbsp. olive or vegetable oil

Serving:

- 3 whole grain hamburg buns or English muffins, toasted
- 3 Tbsp. plain, Sriracha, or wasabi mayonnaise, or tartar sauce (store-bought or homemade from recipe on page 163)

Directions

1. In medium mixing bowl, combine ingredients for patties.
2. Stir mixture with a fork, until salmon is flaked into small pieces and mixture is homogenous.
3. Allow patty mixture to sit for a few minutes and then divide it evenly into thirds.
4. Shape each portion into a ball.
5. Heat a large frying pan over medium heat. Add olive oil to pan.
6. Drop one ball of salmon into the hot hot frying pan and press the ball to flatten it and form a patty about 4" in diameter.
7. Repeat process with other balls.
8. Cook patties until they are lightly browned on the first side (3 – 5 minutes), flip over, and cook until browned on the second side.
9. Remove patties from heat and serve immediately on toasted buns. Top patties with your choice of condiment.

SEAFOOD SALAD

Serves 4 - 6

This Seafood Salad gets a pleasant little kick from the Sriracha mayonnaise. The kick is mild, but if you don't want it at all, use half Sriracha mayonnaise, and half plain mayonnaise. For a no-carb alternative, serve this Seafood Salad atop lettuce leaves.

Ingredients

Salad:

- 1 lb. cooked shrimp (shelled and de-veined)
- two 6 oz. cans lump crabmeat, drained or 8 oz. package lump crab meat
- ¼ cup sliced green onion (1 onion) or finely minced red onion
- ½ cup Sriracha mayonnaise (store-bought or homemade: ½ cup mayonnaise + 1 ½ tsp. Sriracha chili pepper hot sauce)
- 1 Tbsp. snipped fresh chives
- 1 tsp. ground celery seed
- ¼ tsp. salt
- 1 tsp. balsamic vinegar

Serving:

- pita bread, Italian sub rolls, English muffins (toasted; served open-faced), or sliced bread

Directions

1. **For Salad:** Cut shrimp into ¼" slices and transfer to a medium mixing bowl.
2. Add remaining ingredients for salad.
3. Stir until thoroughly mixed.
4. Cover and chill until serving time.
5. **To Serve:** Stuff seafood salad into pita pockets or onto rolls, English muffins, or bread.

SPICY BLACK BEAN BURGERS

Makes 9 burgers

These burgers are vegetarian, but can be made completely vegan by swapping out the eggs for ½ cup of the juice drained off a can of chick peas (yes, really!). Either way, these hearty, spicy burgers will win over all those carnivores who think vegetarian/vegan food = lettuce with a squeeze of lemon juice. Not so!

Ingredients

Burger Mix:

- ½ cup pearl barley
- 1 cup water
- two 15 oz. cans black beans, drained but not rinsed
- 4 oz. can mild, diced green chile peppers
- ½ cup frozen sweet corn
- ½ cup finely minced or grated white or yellow onion (½ of a medium onion)
- 1 Tbsp. finely minced chipotle peppers in adobo sauce (¼ of a 4 oz. can – chop and freeze the rest of the can, for a later use)
- 1 Tbsp. finely minced or pressed garlic (3 large cloves)
- 1 Tbsp. finely minced fresh cilantro
- 1 cup pulverized tortilla chip crumbs (blitz the bits from the bottom of a bag in a blender or food processor)
- 2 large eggs
- 2 tsp. chili powder
- 2 tsp. ground cumin
- 1 tsp. dried oregano
- 1 tsp. salt

Frying:

- 3 Tbsp. olive or vegetable oil

Serving:

- 9 whole grain hamburg buns or English muffins, toasted (optional)
- 8 oz. sliced cheddar cheese
- 2 avocados, peeled, pitted, and thinly sliced
- 1 cup salsa (your choice of type)
- 1 cup sour cream

Directions

1. In a 1-quart saucepan, combine barley and water.
2. Cover, place pot over high heat, and bring to a boil.
3. Stir, reduce heat to low, cover, and allow to simmer (undisturbed) for 15 minutes. Check barley for doneness and remove from heat when tender.
4. While barley is cooking, prepare rest of burger mix. In a large mixing bowl, place drained beans. Mash lightly with a fork, leaving some bits and whole beans.
5. Add remaining ingredients for burgers to beans in bowl.
6. When barley is cooked, add it to the ingredients in the bowl.
7. Mix everything together until thoroughly blended.
8. Portion burger mix using ½ cup measure as a scoop. Shape each portion into a burger that is about 4" in diameter and ½" thick. (Burgers do not shrink, so you can size them to fit any bun.)
9. Heat a large frying pan over medium heat. Add oil for frying.
10. Transfer burgers to frying pan and cook until browned on the bottom (about 5 minutes). Flip burgers over and cook an additional 5 minutes on the second side.
11. Serve burgers on buns or naked, with your choice of toppings.

Note: Spicy Black Bean Burgers may be made ahead and frozen before frying. Wrap each burger individually in plastic wrap, then place all of them in a zip-top freezer bag. Spicy Black Bean Burgers will keep for several months in the freezer. Thaw before frying.

Margherita Pizza, recipe on page 49

PIZZA

I swear, the brick-oven pizza restaurant near my house has me under a spell. Their pizza is amazing. Crust handmade from their own recipe, the dough rolled and tossed thin, finished with just the right amount of toppings and cheese, thrown into a blisteringly hot oven, and then yanked out just before it burns. Oh, my mouth is watering just writing about it.

I fancy myself a great pizza-maker, but what I love most about pizza is how versatile it is, how it lends itself to endless improvisation and creativity. My pizza and your pizza and their pizza can all be incredible, and wildly different from one another. I don't own a brick oven (I know, so sad) so I can't make the restaurant's pizza, but I can make a killer Chicago-Style Deep Dish (recipe included in this chapter). My hope is that my recipes will inspire you to create from-scratch pizzas all your own.

CHICAGO-STYLE DEEP DISH PIZZA

Makes three 9" round or two 9" x 13" deep-dish pizzas; serves 6-10

When we moved from Chicago to the East Coast, I was incredibly glad I had perfected this recipe while living in the pizza mecca that is Chicago. This recipe has spared me much homesickness and pizza longing, as I now live in a place with no idea what real pizza is. This pizza takes three hours to make from start-to-finish (part of that time is for the dough to rise, so you do get a break) and it serves a crowd (or an incredibly hungry few), so plan accordingly.

Ingredients

Crust:

- 1 ¼ cup milk warmed to 105°-115° (should feel like warm bath water)
- 1 packet active dry yeast (2 ¼ tsp.)
- ½ cup olive oil
- 1 tsp. salt
- 1 cup grated Parmesan cheese
- 1 cup corn meal
- ½ cup whole wheat flour
- 2 ½ cups bread flour

Toppings for three pizzas:

- 1 ½ to 2 lbs. mozzarella cheese (sliced is best, but shredded is okay)
- "meat(s)" of your choice (pre-cook any raw meats), about 4-6 oz. per kind, per pizza
- diced or sliced veggies of your choice (pre-cook and drain mushrooms, broccoli, eggplant, and zucchini, if using), 1-2 cups total per pizza
- two 28 oz. cans diced tomatoes, drained (drink juice or reserve for another use)
- 6 oz. can tomato paste
- 3 tsp. dried basil
- 3 tsp. finely minced or pressed garlic (3 large cloves)
- 3 Tbsp. olive oil (optional)

Directions

1. **For Crust:** In a large mixing bowl, combine warm milk and yeast. Stir with a sturdy wooden spoon and allow to sit for 5 minutes for yeast to dissolve and get foamy.
2. Add oil and salt and mix in.
3. In a pile on the counter, mix cheese with cornmeal. Add mixture to bowl along with wheat flour and 1 cup of bread flour. Mix until a smooth dough forms.
4. Add remaining bread flour and mix in as much as you can with the spoon. Using hands, knead remaining flour into dough.
5. Transfer dough to work surface and knead for an additional couple minutes after all the flour is incorporated, to make the dough smooth and elastic.
6. Grease the mixing bowl with oil or spray oil, and return dough to bowl. Turn and flip dough so all sides are covered with oil.
7. Cover bowl with a damp towel and set aside to rise for one hour.
8. **For Toppings:** While dough is rising, prepare all toppings. Chop all "meats" and vegetables and pre-cook those that require it.
9. Prepare tomato sauce by combining drained tomatoes and tomato paste in a medium mixing bowl. Stir to combine.
10. **To Assemble:** When dough is ready, punch it down to deflate it, and divide it into three equal portions for round pizzas, or two equal portions for 9" x 13" pizzas.
11. Press each portion into the bottom of a baking pan (springform pans or cake pans for round pizzas) and up 1" high on the sides. If dough resists you, let it rest for 5 minutes to relax, then try again.
12. Pierce crusts all over with a fork (pricks about 1" apart).
13. Preheat oven to 425° and allow crusts to rise for 15 minutes while oven heats up.
14. Do not place any toppings on crusts at this time.

15. **For Baking:** When crusts have risen and oven is up to temperature, place crusts in oven and bake them for 7 minutes.
16. Remove crusts from oven and add toppings as quickly as you possibly can, in the following order: cheese (lay out slices to cover bottom of crusts), "meats" and veggies, and then the tomato mixture (divide contents of bowl between the pizzas).
17. Sprinkle basil and garlic over top of tomatoes and drizzle a small amount of olive oil over each pizza (if desired).
18. Return pizzas to the oven and bake an additional 20–30 minutes. When done, pizzas will be golden brown around the edges and crust will have pulled away from the sides of the pan a little bit.
19. Remove pizzas from pans, cut into wedges or squares, and serve.

Excellent topping combinations:

- **Greek:** spinach + thinly sliced artichoke hearts + sliced black olives + sliced onions + part feta cheese + a sprinkle of dried oregano on top
- **Veggie Lovers:** spinach + diced eggplant + broccoli florets + sliced mushrooms + sliced onions + roasted peppers
- **Sausage:** veggie sausage + sliced onions
- **Supreme:** veggie pepperoni + veggie sausage + veggie bacon + sliced green bell peppers + sliced onions + sliced olives
- **Smoked Salmon:** smoked salmon + veggie bacon + sliced mushrooms + part goat cheese
- **Shrimp:** shrimp + diced zucchini + sliced mushrooms + extra garlic + part Parmesan cheese

CALZONES

Makes 4; serves 2-4

Calzones are essentially small pizzas that have been folded in half with the toppings on the inside. Pizza sauce is served on the side as a dipping sauce. Ricotta cheese is essential for calzone authenticity, so please don't make these without it!

Ingredients

Crust:
- 1 cup water warmed to 105°–115° (should feel like warm bath water)
- 1 tsp. granulated sugar
- 1 packet active dry yeast (2 ¼ tsp.)
- ¼ cup olive oil
- 1 tsp. salt
- 3 cups bread flour (1 cup whole wheat flour + 2 cups bread flour for whole grain crust)

Cheeses:
- 8 oz. carton ricotta cheese (1 cup)
- 8 oz. package grated mozzarella cheese (2 cups)

Toppings/Fillings:
- your choice of "meats" and/or veggies, up to ½ cup per calzone (pre-cook all raw "meats," and any vegetables that don't cook quickly or that release a lot of liquid when cooked, like mushrooms, zucchini, eggplant, broccoli, etc.)
- 2 tsp. dried basil (optional)

Serving:
- 1 cup pizza sauce for dipping (store-bought or homemade from recipe on page 161)

Suggested topping combinations:
- veggie sausage + veggie pepperoni + sliced onions + sliced bell peppers
- fresh spinach + sliced olives + fresh diced tomatoes + fresh minced garlic
- sliced mushrooms + broccoli florets + roasted peppers + fresh minced garlic
- pan-fried veggie chik'n cutlet, sliced + veggie bacon + sliced onions or mushrooms
- cooked shrimp + zucchini + mushrooms

Directions

1. **For Dough:** In a medium mixing bowl, combine water, sugar, and yeast.
2. Stir and let sit for 5 minutes (yeast should get foamy).
3. Add oil, salt, and 2 ½ cups of the flour. Stir until well mixed and formed into a lumpy ball.
4. Dump remaining ½ cup flour on a clean countertop and place the ball of dough on top. Knead the dough until all the flour is incorporated and dough is smooth and elastic.
5. Grease the mixing bowl with olive oil, and place the dough in the bowl, turning the dough over so all sides are oiled.
6. Set dough aside and allow to rise for 1 hour.
7. **Toppings/Fillings:** All raw "meats" and some veggies need to be sliced or diced and pre-cooked. Prep fillings while dough is rising.
8. **To Assemble:** Preheat oven to 400°.
9. Punch crust dough down and divide into four equal pieces.
10. Roll each portion of dough out to an 8" circle (10" if you want your calzones to have a thin crust).
11. Top half of each circle of dough with ¼ cup ricotta cheese, spreading the cheese evenly but keeping it 1" away from the edge of the dough.
12. Top this with mozzarella cheese (½ cup per calzone), and your choice of toppings.
13. Fold the circle of dough in half, pulling the plain half over the toppings.
14. Press the edges of dough together. Seal the edges by rolling the edge back over itself and pressing firmly to stick it down.
15. Transfer finished calzones to a lightly oiled baking sheet, and brush tops with olive oil. Prick each calzone in the center top with a knife, to make a tiny vent hole. If making calzones with different fillings in them, make the prick marks distinctive, so you can tell the calzones apart once they are baked.
16. Bake calzones for 20 minutes. Serve calzones hot with pizza sauce on the side for dipping.

MARGHERITA PIZZA

Makes one 16" thin crust pizza; serves 2-4

I think of this as a "summer only" pizza because the flavor is best with garden-fresh tomatoes and basil. Also, it whips up quick and is much lighter fare than a traditional pizza. If you want to really ramp up the flavor, spread 2–3 Tbsp. pesto sauce in place of the olive oil on the crust.

Ingredients

Crust:

- ½ cup water warmed to 105°–115° (should feel like warm bath water)
- 1 tsp. active dry yeast (1 packet = 2 ¼ tsp.)
- ½ tsp. salt
- ½ cup semolina flour
- ¾ cup bread flour

Toppings:

- 1 Tbsp. olive oil
- 1 clove of garlic, finely minced
- 2-3 large beefsteak tomatoes, cored and cut into thin slices (no more than ¼" thick)
- 8 oz. fresh mozzarella, sliced ¼" thick
- 2 Tbsp. finely shredded fresh basil leaves

Directions

1. **For Crust:** In a medium mixing bowl, sprinkle yeast over water. Stir with a sturdy wooden spoon and allow to sit for 5 minutes for yeast to dissolve.
2. Add salt and flours and mix in, using hands after dough is too stiff for the spoon.
3. Turn dough out onto a counter and knead for a minute by rolling the ball of dough around under the palm of your hand until it is smooth.
4. Grease the mixing bowl with oil or spray oil, and return dough to bowl. Turn and flip dough so all sides of dough are covered with oil.
5. Cover bowl with a damp towel and set aside to rise for one to two hours.
6. **To Assemble:** When dough has doubled in size, punch it down to deflate it, and use a rolling pin to flatten the dough into a cracker-thin crust, 16" in diameter. If the dough is too elastic and resists rolling to this thinness, let dough rest for 5-10 minutes and try again.
7. Lightly grease a pizza pan or baking sheet. Transfer circle of dough onto it, and stretch the dough back to a 16" diameter.
8. Preheat oven to 450°.
9. Brush olive oil over crust.
10. Sprinkle garlic over oil.
11. Completely cover crust with tomato slices.
12. Lay mozzarella slices over top of tomatoes, distributing evenly.
13. Scatter strips of basil over top of pizza.
14. Bake pizza for 18-20 minutes, until cheese is golden brown on top.
15. Remove from oven, allow to cool for a few minutes, slice into wedges, and serve.

Margherita Pizza is pictured on page 45

MEXICAN PIZZA

Makes one 16" thin crust pizza; serves 2-4

Unusual and a great alternative for Taco Tuesday!

Ingredients

Crust:

- ¾ cup water warmed to 105°-115° (should feel like warm bath water)
- 1 packet active dry yeast (2 ¼ tsp.)
- ½ tsp. salt
- ¼ cup olive oil
- ½ cup instant corn Masa flour (for tortillas) or cornmeal
- ½ cup semolina flour (substitute bread flour if semolina is unavailable)
- 1 cup bread flour

Toppings:

- 15 oz. can refried beans (2 cups)
- 8 oz. jar salsa or picante sauce (1 cup)
- 8 oz. package grated mozzarella, Monterey Jack, or pepper jack cheese (2 cups)
- 2.25 oz. can sliced olives, drained (½ cup)
- 1 cup sliced green onions
- 1 cup diced beefsteak tomato or halved cherry tomatoes (½ pint)
- 1 Tbsp. coarsely chopped fresh cilantro

Condiments (optional):

- 1 cup sour cream
- 2 avocados, peeled, pitted, and diced

Directions

1. **For Crust:** In a medium mixing bowl, sprinkle yeast over water. Stir with a sturdy wooden spoon and allow to sit for 5 minutes for yeast to dissolve.
2. Add salt, oil, Masa, and semolina flour. Mix in, using hands after dough is too stiff for the spoon.
3. Add remaining flour, and mix in with hands. Knead dough until flour is thoroughly incorporated and dough is smooth and elastic (about 5 minutes).
4. Grease the mixing bowl with oil or spray oil, and return dough to bowl. Turn and flip dough so all sides of dough are covered with oil.
5. Cover bowl with a damp towel and set aside to rise for one hour.
6. **To Assemble:** Preheat oven to 425°.
7. Punch down dough for crust, transfer to a work surface, and roll out into a 16" circle.
8. Place circle of dough on a pizza pan or baking sheet.
9. Spread beans evenly over crust.
10. Top beans with salsa and then cheese, distributing each evenly.
11. Sprinkle olives, onions, tomatoes, and cilantro over all.
12. Bake pizza for 20-25 minutes, until crust is golden brown.
13. Remove from oven and cut into wedges. If desired, serve with dollops of sour cream and diced avocado on top.

SICILIAN PIZZA

Makes 13" x 18" sheet pan or two 9" x 13" pans; serves 8-12

Sicilian pizza features a thick crust and is "traditionally" topped with mozzarella and pepperoni, or no cheese and caramelized onions, or Italian caciocavallo cheese and anchovies. Whatever your tradition, my pizza is old-school plain cheese and calls for the sauce on the bottom with cheese on top. Certainly, you can make it with cheese on the bottom and sauce on top, or add toppings of your choosing, or replace the cheese with whatever you choose, but this is my cookbook, so this is Sicilian pizza done my way!

Ingredients

Crust:
- 1 ¼ cups water warmed to 105°-115° (should feel like warm bath water)
- 1 packet active dry yeast (2 ¼ tsp.)
- ¼ cup olive oil
- 3 ½ cups bread flour (1 ½ cups whole wheat flour + 2 cups bread flour for wholegrain crust)
- 2 tsp. salt

Pan:
- ¼ cup olive oil

Sauce:
- 1 cup pizza sauce (8 oz. jar store-bought, or homemade from recipe on page 161)

Toppings:
- 8 oz. fresh mozzarella
- 16-24 oz. shredded mozzarella cheese (4-6 cups)

Directions

1. **For Crust:** In a medium mixing bowl, sprinkle yeast over water. Stir with a sturdy wooden spoon and allow to sit for 5 minutes for yeast to dissolve.
2. Add oil, flour, and salt. Mix in, using hands after dough is too stiff for the spoon.
3. Turn dough out onto a work surface and knead for 2 minutes more, until dough is smooth and elastic.
4. Spread the ¼ cup olive oil out on a rimmed 13" x 18" baking sheet.
5. Lay the dough on top of the oil and turn it over, to coat the dough in oil.
6. With hands, spread the dough out to fill the pan as much as possible (dough will be too elastic to stretch all the way).
7. Cover dough with plastic wrap and allow to rise for 2 hours. While dough is rising, make pizza sauce if using homemade. If adding any toppings, prep those too.
8. **To Assemble:** Remove plastic from crust dough. With hands, very gently stretch the dough out to fill the pan completely, being careful not to press the air bubbles out of the dough.
9. Set crust aside for 20 minutes (uncovered), for it to rise again.
10. Preheat oven to 450°.
11. Spoon pizza sauce onto crust. With the back of the spoon, gently spread sauce to an even thickness.
12. Rip fresh mozzarella into small pieces and scatter pieces across pizza, on top of the sauce.
13. Spread shredded mozzarella evenly over pizza.
14. Bake pizza for 20-25 minutes, until cheese is golden brown on top.
15. Remove pizza from oven, allow to cool for 5 minutes, cut into squares, and serve.

WHITE PIZZA

Makes one 10" deep-dish pizza; serves 2–4

Rich and oh-so-very-good, this unusual pizza features an Alfredo sauce instead of the traditional tomato-based sauce. It is both a delightful change-of-pace and a delicious addition to a pizza buffet.

Ingredients

Crust:

- ½ cup water warmed to 105°–115° (should feel like warm bath water)
- 1 tsp. active dry yeast (1 packet = 2 ¼ tsp.)
- ¼ cup olive oil
- 3 cloves garlic, finely minced or pressed (1 Tbsp.)
- 1 tsp. dried garlic powder
- ½ tsp. salt
- 2 cups bread flour

Alfredo Sauce:

- 2 Tbsp. butter
- 3 oz. smoky tempeh or other veggie bacon, diced
- ½ cup heavy cream
- 1 cup grated Parmesan cheese
- 1 Tbsp. minced parsley (fresh or dried)

Toppings:

- 12 oz. mozzarella cheese, sliced or shredded (3 cups)
- 4 oz. can sliced mushrooms, drained
- 1 cup thinly sliced white or yellow onion (1 small onion)
- 1 tsp. finely minced garlic (1 large clove)

Directions

1. **For Crust:** In medium mixing bowl, sprinkle yeast over water. Stir with a sturdy wooden spoon and allow to sit for 5 minutes for yeast to dissolve.
2. Add remaining crust ingredients. Mix in, using hands after dough is too stiff for the spoon.
3. Turn dough out onto a counter and knead for several minutes, until the dough is smooth and elastic.
4. Return dough to bowl. Cover bowl with a damp towel and set aside for dough to rise for one to two hours.
5. **For Sauce:** Prepare sauce while dough is rising. In a 1-quart saucepan over medium heat, melt the butter.
6. Add the tempeh. Fry the tempeh until lightly browned and slightly crispy, stirring occasionally (5–10 minutes).
7. Add the cream and heat the sauce just to a simmer (steam will rise off cream and small bubbles will form around the edge of the mixture. Do not allow cream to boil).
8. Add Parmesan cheese and parsley. Stir. Cook just until mixture returns to a simmer. Remove sauce from heat and set aside.
9. **Toppings:** Prepare toppings while dough is rising.
10. **To Assemble:** Preheat oven to 425°.
11. After dough for crust has doubled in size, punch it down to deflate it. Transfer dough to a lightly greased 10" springform pan, 10" cast iron skillet, or equivalent baking pan.
12. Pat and stretch dough to fill bottom of pan, then press dough further to go 1" up the sides of the pan. Let crust rest for 5 minutes. Prick crust all over with a fork (pricks 1" apart).
14. Bake crust for 7 minutes.
15. Remove crust from oven. Working quickly, pour sauce into crust and spread to an even thickness.
16. Top sauce with cheese, distributing it evenly.
17. Top cheese with remaining toppings, in the order listed.
18. Return pizza to oven and bake for 25–30 minutes more, until the crust is golden brown and has pulled away from the sides of the pan. Remove pizza from oven, slice in wedges, and serve.

White Pizza is pictured in Table of Contents

QUICK AND EASY ENTREES

I love to cook but not every day. And sometimes, I'm in the mood to cook but don't have much time. My favorite cheat is Movie Night, which involves popcorn, cheese, and fruit for dinner in front of the TV. Before you judge, I do have standards, and I do have rules: the popcorn has to be made on the stove (no microwave, no space-age appliances) and seasoned (cheesy, veggie bacon-bitty, dry Ranch-y); it only counts as dinner if the cheese is fancy (cheese curds, smoked gouda, drunken goat, horseradish cheddar, gorgonzola, etc.); and the fruit must be real (apple slices, grapes, dried dates, etc. — no fruit roll-ups or strawberry ice cream).

When we've already had a Movie Night, and a second fit of dinnertime "I don't wanna cook" strikes in the same week, I turn to the recipes in this chapter. They are as advertised: quick and easy, plus tasty to boot.

30-MINUTE CHILI

Serves 6-8

Traditional chili benefits from a long, slow simmer for the flavors to develop and meld. This recipe employs canned products that have done their simmering in the canning process and are ready to join forces for a great, quick chili.

Ingredients

Chili:

- 15 oz. can kidney beans, drained and rinsed
- 15 oz. can black beans, drained and rinsed
- two 28 oz. cans diced tomatoes
- 16 oz. jar salsa (your choice of type and heat level)
- 6 oz. can tomato paste
- 4 oz. can diced mild green chile peppers
- 12 oz. package ground veggie soy crumbles
- 1 Tbsp. chili powder
- 1 tsp. dried oregano
- ½ tsp. ground cumin
- 1 tsp. salt
- ½ tsp. ground black pepper

Toppings:

- 8 oz. grated cheddar cheese
- ½ cup sour cream

Directions

1. In a 4-quart stock pot, dump all ingredients for chili.
2. Stir, cover, and place over medium heat.
3. Bring to a boil, reduce heat to low, and simmer for 5-10 minutes.
4. Serve chili hot in individual bowls, topped with grated cheese and a dollop of sour cream.

BAKED LEMON-GARLIC FISH

Serves 4-8

Simply spectacular and done in a flash! Serve with sliced bread and a tossed salad for a super-quick meal.

Ingredients

Fish:

- 2 lbs. whitefish filets (tilapia, flounder, cod, orange roughy, or other)

Sauce:

- 3 large cloves garlic (1 Tbsp.), minced and smashed into a paste with ½ tsp. salt
- 1 tsp. dried oregano
- ½ tsp. dried basil
- ¼ tsp. dried rosemary
- ¼ tsp. ground black pepper
- ¼ cup lemon juice (2 lemons)
- 2 Tbsp. olive oil

Directions

1. Preheat oven to 350°.
2. Lay fish out flat in the bottom of a 9" x 13" non-reactive baking pan (no aluminum).
3. **For Sauce:** In a small bowl, combine all ingredients for sauce. Mix with a whisk until emulsified.
4. Pour sauce over fish.
5. Bake fish for 10–15 minutes, until fish is firm and flakes when you press on it.
6. Serve fish hot with a little sauce spooned over top.

CREAMY PESTO ORZO WITH SHRIMP

Makes 9" x 13" pan; serves 6-8

Cooking raw pasta by baking it is my new favorite thing. It takes longer than boiling but requires so much less work and dirties so many fewer dishes, the trade-off is a win in my book. And for people in drought-stricken areas, this way of cooking pasta also requires no water. This casserole comes together in 5 minutes — literally—and leaves you free to do something else while dinner takes care of itself, deliciously bubbling away in the oven.

Ingredients

- 16 oz. package dry orzo pasta (3 cups)
- two 7 oz. jars pesto sauce or 2 cups homemade pesto
- 2 lbs. raw shrimp, peeled and deveined (any size)
- 16 oz. package frozen broccoli, thawed, or 2 heads fresh broccoli, cut into small pieces
- 1 pint cherry tomatoes, halved (2 cups)
- ½ tsp. salt
- 2 cups milk

Directions

1. Preheat oven to 350°.
2. In a 9" x 13" baking pan, combine orzo and pesto sauce. Stir to combine. Spread to an even thickness in the bottom of the pan.
3. Top orzo with a layer of shrimp, then a layer of broccoli, and finally a layer of tomatoes.
4. Sprinkle salt over all.
5. Pour milk over top.
6. Cover pan with a tight-fitting lid or two thicknesses of aluminum foil, sealed tightly.
7. Bake for 60 minutes.
8. Remove from oven, stir, and serve.

GARLIC SHRIMP

Serves 4-6

This is one of my favorite go-to recipes for a quick dinner. The shrimp are done in minutes but taste like I fussed. Add tortillas, lettuce, and a bit of Ranch or Caesar dressing to the menu, and you will have the best shrimp wraps ever. Or skip the tortillas and throw together a shrimp Caesar salad.

Ingredients

- 1 lb. raw shrimp, peeled and deveined
- ½ cup sliced green onions (2-3 onions)
- 3 large cloves garlic, minced and smashed to a paste with ¼ tsp. salt (1 Tbsp.)
- ¼ cup grated fresh Parmesan cheese
- 2 Tbsp. olive oil

Directions

1. Preheat oven to 350°.
2. In a medium mixing bowl, combine all ingredients.
3. Transfer shrimp mixture to an 8" square baking pan (or equivalent) and spread to an even layer.
4. Bake shrimp for 15-20 minutes, depending on the size of the shrimp. Shrimp will be opaque and firm to the touch when done. Be careful not to over-cook the shrimp as they will become tough and rubbery.

KIELBASA AND POTATOES

Serves 4-6

This recipe started out as campfire food and can still be made that way: cut the potatoes into smaller 1" pieces and assemble the ingredients into individual pouches made of heavy-duty aluminum foil, making sure to put the onions on the bottom. Seal the pouches well and toss them into the coals of a campfire or fire in the fireplace (avoid using the hottest area of the fire, or things will burn before cooking through). Check for doneness after about 20 minutes.

Ingredients

- 1 large yellow or white onion, sliced (about 2 cups)
- 6 fist-sized potatoes (any variety), or equivalent volume of other sizes
- 12 oz. package veggie kielbasa
- 1 cup vegetable broth store-bought, homemade, or 1 cup water + 1 tsp. Better Than Bouillon (vegetable or vegetarian chicken flavor)

Condiments:

- butter
- sour cream
- yellow and/or brown mustard

Directions

1. In a large covered frying pan, lay sliced onions out in an even layer.
2. Scrub potatoes (do not peel) and cut in half.
3. Place potato pieces, cut side down, on top of onions.
4. Cut kielbasa into 1" thick slices and lay on top of potatoes.
5. Pour broth over all.
6. Cover pan and place over medium heat.
7. Bring to a boil, reduce heat to low, and allow pot to steam and simmer until potatoes are tender (20-30 minutes).
8. Serve hot with condiments, if desired (butter and sour cream for the potatoes, mustard for the kielbasa).

QUICK MACARONI AND CHEESE

Serves 4-6

This cookbook hardly needs one more mac-'n-cheese recipe, but it was impossible for me to choose one to leave out, as they are all different and so tasty! This recipe is by far the fastest and easiest — it employs so many shortcuts that it takes less than 5 minutes to whip up and toss in the oven. And while it bakes, you can catch a quick nap or help kids with their homework, as this dish requires no fussing. If you want to reduce the time involved even further, mix this in the morning and stash it in the fridge until dinnertime. A "soaked" mac-'n-cheese will bake in half the time.

Ingredients

Pasta:

- 2 cups dry macaroni pasta or 2 ½ cups shells, rotini, penne, or rigatoni (8 oz.)
- 2 cups grated sharp or extra-sharp cheddar cheese (8 oz.)

Sauce:

- 15 oz. jar Alfredo sauce
- 1 Alfredo jar full of milk (cover and shake, to rinse jar)

Topping:

- ¼ cup grated Parmesan cheese or ½ cup grated cheddar cheese or 2.8 oz. can French's Fried Onions

Directions

1. Preheat oven to 400°.
2. In a large mixing bowl, toss dry pasta and cheese together.
3. Transfer pasta mixture to an 8" square baking pan (or its equivalent) and spread to an even thickness.
4. In the same mixing bowl, combine Alfredo sauce and milk. Stir with a whisk until smooth and homogenous (about 10 seconds).
5. Pour sauce over pasta mixture in pan.
6. Lightly press on surface of pasta to submerge pieces in the sauce.
7. Cover pan with a tight-fitting lid or a double-layer of aluminum foil.
8. Bake for 40 minutes.
9. Uncover baking pan, stir pasta well (scrape bottom of pan), sprinkle topping on, and return pan (uncovered) to oven for 10 minutes more. Serve hot.

SALMON WITH HONEY-MUSTARD GLAZE

Serves 4

This recipe is a little deceiving — the glaze has a kick of heat from the dry mustard. The sweet-hot combination is just lovely on salmon.

Ingredients

Salmon:

- 2 lbs. salmon steaks or fillets
- Salt and pepper

Honey-Mustard Glaze:

- 1 Tbsp. Colman's dry mustard
- 1 Tbsp. raw or granulated sugar
- 4 tsp. honey
- 1 tsp. water
- ½ tsp. soy sauce

Directions

1. Preheat oven to 350°.
2. Pat salmon dry with a paper towel.
3. Place salmon on a greased baking sheet (skin side down for fillets).
4. Sprinkle lightly with salt and pepper.
5. **For Glaze:** Mix all ingredients together in a small bowl or mug until a smooth paste is formed.
6. Spread glaze on salmon thickly. Glaze should be about ⅛" thick and used up.
7. Bake salmon for 10–12 minutes. Test for doneness by pressing on the salmon in the thickest area. It will flake apart when done. Do not overcook.
8. Honey-mustard glaze may be made ahead in a large batch and frozen. It does not freeze solid, so you can scoop out what you need each time.
9. **Variation:** For a milder result, mix honey-mustard glaze half-and-half with mayonnaise.

SHRIMP FRIED RICE

Serves 4

If you have the ingredients for this dish on hand, you can make it and be eating it before a delivery person could get there with fried rice from your local Chinese restaurant. No kidding. And this stuff is way better, so it will win you bragging rights!

Ingredients

Rice:
- 3 cups leftover brown rice, chilled (1 cup raw + 2 cups water)
- 3 Tbsp. soy sauce
- 1 Tbsp. sesame oil

Eggs:
- 1 Tbsp. butter or vegetable oil
- 2 eggs, lightly beaten

Shrimp:
- 1 Tbsp. sesame oil
- 1 small white or yellow onion, thinly sliced (about 1 cup)
- ½ cup shelled edamame or frozen peas
- ½ tsp. ground ginger
- ½ tsp. garlic powder
- 16 oz. package cooked shrimp, peeled and deveined

Directions

1. Prep all ingredients before beginning to prepare this dish, as it cooks and comes together very quickly and you will need everything at hand.
2. In a medium mixing bowl, combine rice, soy sauce, and sesame oil. Fluff rice and stir mixture to fully incorporate seasonings.
3. Place a large frying pan over medium-high heat (7 on a scale of 1 to 10).
4. When pan is hot, add butter for eggs. Swirl the pan to coat the bottom with butter.
5. Add eggs to pan.
6. Swirl pan so that eggs form a thin layer. Return pan to burner.
7. When eggs puff up (takes just a minute or two) flip them over, and cook on second side for only 30 seconds.
8. Remove eggs from pan and cut into ½" pieces.
9. In the same frying pan over medium-high heat, add the 1 Tbsp. sesame oil. Swirl pan to coat bottom.
10. Add onions, edamame, ginger, and garlic powder. Cook until onions are translucent (about 5 minutes), stirring almost constantly.
11. Add shrimp, rice, and cooked eggs. Stir to combine.
12. Cook mixture just until heated through, stirring almost constantly. Taste, adjust seasonings, and serve.

SLOPPY JOES

Makes 8 sloppy joes

This vegetarian take on the classic is surprisingly "meaty!" Quick to whip up when time is tight, sloppy joes are just the thing to make for a mid-week family dinner.

Ingredients

Joes:

- 12 oz. package ground veggie soy crumbles
- 15 oz. can lentils, drained (or 2 cups cooked lentils)
- 16 oz. jar salsa (2 cups any variety except chipotle pepper), puréed in a blender or food processor.
- ½ cup ketchup
- 4 Tbsp. tomato paste (½ of a 6 oz. can)
- 2 Tbsp. brown sugar
- 2 Tbsp. vegetarian Worcestershire sauce
- ½ tsp. salt

Serving:

- 8 whole grain buns
- 8 oz. sliced cheddar, mozzarella, or American cheese (optional)

Directions

1. In a 2-quart saucepan, combine all ingredients for sloppy joes.
2. Cover, place over medium heat, and bring to a simmer.
3. Reduce heat to low. Simmer for 10 minutes, stirring often.
4. Serve sloppy joe mixture on buns, topped with cheese, if desired.

TONY MACARONI

Serves 4–6

Growing up, my mother made a noodle casserole she called Jon-Ben-Getty. I have no idea where the name or the recipe came from, but that casserole was a family favorite. Jon-Ben-Getty pre-dated the arrival of Hamburger Helper on store shelves, but it had a lot in common with that more famous dish. In addition to ground beef, my mother's casserole featured heavily processed foods (like canned soups and Velveeta cheese) which made it quick to throw together but not particularly healthy. Missing ol' Jon one day, I created a healthy knock-off of the cheesy, noodle-y casserole of my youth. I have fondly dubbed it "Tony Macaroni," as I think my Tony and my mother's Mr. Jon-Ben-Getty could be friends.

Ingredients

- 1 red bell pepper, seeded and cut in large pieces (if you use a green bell pepper instead, the appetizing color of the finished dish will be compromised)
- 1 medium yellow or white onion, peeled and cut in large pieces (about 1 ½ cups)
- 2 large cloves garlic (2 tsp.)
- 2 cups milk
- 12 oz. package ground veggie soy crumbles
- 2 cups whole grain dry elbow macaroni pasta or 2 ½ cups penne (8 oz.)
- 1 tsp. chili powder
- 1 tsp. paprika (sweet, not hot)
- 1 tsp. salt
- 8 oz. package shredded cheddar cheese (2 cups)

Directions

1. In the container of a blender or food processor fitted with a steel blade, combine pepper, onion, garlic, and milk. Puree until veggies are in bits.
2. Transfer pepper mixture to a 3-quart, deep skillet over medium-high heat.
3. Add remaining ingredients, except cheese. Cover.
4. Bring mixture to a boil, stirring occasionally.
5. Reduce heat to medium-low (4 on a scale of 1 to 10.) Simmer for 7–10 minutes, until the macaroni is al dente. Stir once or twice during cooking.
6. Add the cheese to the skillet. Stir in. Taste, adjust seasonings, and serve.

WASABI TUNA STEAKS

Serves 4

I love tuna steaks for nights when dinner needs to be ready right now. On those nights, my go-to plan of action is to wash some potatoes, prick them, get them cooking in the microwave, and put a frying pan on to heat while I prep Wasabi Tuna Steaks. With a quick vegetable — sliced beefsteak tomatoes from my garden! — I have a fantastic dinner on the table in 10 minutes. Seriously.

Ingredients

- 1 lb. thick-cut tuna steaks (four 4 oz. steaks)

Seasoning:

- 2 tsp. soy sauce
- 2 tsp. wasabi powder (available at spice shops or online)
- ¼ tsp. salt
- ½ tsp. ground black pepper

Frying:

- 2 tsp. sesame oil or vegetable oil

Directions

1. Place a large cast iron skillet or other heavy frying pan over medium-high heat (7 on a scale of 1 to 10). Allow pan to get smoking hot while you season the fish.
2. Lay tuna steaks out on a plate. Sprinkle with soy sauce.
3. Combine the wasabi powder, salt, and pepper in a small ramekin or mug. Stir to combine.
4. Sprinkle half the dry seasonings over one side of the tuna steaks, distributing seasoning evenly.
5. When pan is hot, add oils, and swirl pan to coat bottom.
6. Quickly transfer fish to hot pan, seasoned side down.
7. Cook on first side for 45 seconds. While fish is cooking on first side, sprinkle remaining seasoning mix on top side of steaks.
8. Flip fish immediately. Cook for 45 seconds on second side, remove from pan, and serve.

Tuscan Stuffed Mahi Mahi, recipe on page 78

FISH ENTREES

Growing up, my mother was a midwestern meat-and-potatoes kind of cook who had but two ways of preparing fish. If we were vacationing on a lake and caught fish (usually perch, sunfish, or pike), she would dredge the fresh filets in seasoned flour and fry them in melted Crisco. She was always in a hurry, not very interested in cooking while on vacation, so the fish was fried just barely enough and was amazingly, incredibly delicious. If we were home, however, Fish Night meant this recipe: Take a 9" x 13" pan and pour ½ cup (1 stick) of melted margarine into it. Lay cod filets on top. Sprinkle with paprika. Bake in 350° oven for 100 days. It was, as you might imagine, not delicious.

It took time and one great meal for me to get over my fear of Fish Night. The meal was the rehearsal dinner for my wedding. My husband's oldest brother lived in Alaska, was an avid hunter and fisherman, and brought a suitcase full of frozen, wild-caught salmon filets with him to the wedding weekend in Michigan. He thawed the fish, marinated it, and grilled it to mouth-watering perfection for the rehearsal dinner. Everyone raved. I was in awe. I had no idea fish could taste like that.

Since then, I have expanded my own Fish Night repertoire to include a much greater variety of fish and manners of preparation. This chapter is my edible gift to you — grab a recipe and actually enjoy a Fish Night!

BEER BATTERED FISH

Serves 4

I struggled for years to find or invent a recipe for good, beer-battered fish, to no avail. Everything I tried was terrible in one way or another, until I stumbled on this, which is the simplest thing: equal quantities of beer and self-rising flour. Eureka! This batter also makes tasty onion rings.

Ingredients

Oil:
- 8 cups vegetable oil for deep frying (64 oz.)

Fish:
- 2 lbs. haddock, cod, or flounder fillets
- salt and pepper

Batter:
- 1 ½ cups self-rising flour (or 1 ½ cups all-purpose flour + 2 ½ tsp. baking powder + ¼ tsp. salt
- 12 oz. bottle of beer (any will do, but not super-dark)

Serving:
- ½ cup seafood cocktail sauce (store-bought or homemade from recipe on page 164)
- ½ cup tartar sauce (store-bought or homemade from recipe on page 163) or ½ cup skordalia from recipe on page 162

Directions

1. **For Frying:** In a stockpot, deep frying pan, electric fryer, or wok, heat oil to 375° (a deep-fry thermometer is invaluable). Oil should be at least 3" deep. Line a baking sheet with several layers of paper towels or newspaper, lay a cooling rack upside down on top of paper, and set aside.
2. Preheat a warming oven to 200°.
3. **For Fish:** Pat fish dry and season lightly with salt and pepper.
4. In a small mixing bowl, combine flour and beer and stir with a fork or whisk until combined.
5. When oil is up to temperature, dip fish in batter, let excess run off, and then drop battered fish into oil. Cook fish in several batches to avoid over-crowding oil.
6. Cook fish for about 5 minutes, flipping pieces over in the middle of cooking time.
7. Remove fish from oil when golden brown, using tongs or a spider strainer, and place on prepared tray to drain.
8. Place tray in oven to stay warm.
9. Allow oil to come back up to temperature before adding next batch of fish.
10. Serve fish hot, with seafood cocktail sauce and/or tartar sauce and/or skordalia on the side for dipping.

FISH CURRY

Serves 4

This is one of my favorite shortcut-to-Indian-food-deliciousness recipes. It is quick enough for a weekday meal, and fantastic enough for company.

Ingredients

Fish:

- 1 lb. cod or other firm, whitefish fillets (if filets are large, cut into four serving-sized portions)

Spice Blend:

- 1 tsp. Colman's dry mustard
- 1 tsp. ground cumin
- 1 tsp. ground coriander
- 1 tsp. ground ginger or 1 Tbsp. fresh ginger root, peeled and grated on a microplane or the finest side of a box grater
- 1 tsp. salt
- 1 tsp. granulated sugar
- ½ tsp. garam masala (store-bought, or from recipe on page 151)
- ½ tsp. ground turmeric
- ⅛ tsp. cayenne pepper (up to ½ tsp. for extreme heat)

Sauce:

- 2 Tbsp. peanut or vegetable oil
- 1 medium white or yellow onion, finely minced (about 1 ½ cups)
- 4 large cloves garlic, finely minced or pressed (4 tsp.)
- 1 cup diced tomato (fresh or canned)

Garnish:

- ½ cup chopped cashews
- ¼ cup chopped fresh cilantro

Directions

1. Preheat oven to 350°.
2. Lay fish fillets in an 8" square baking dish (or equivalent) and set aside.
3. **For Spice Blend:** Combine all ingredients for spice blend in a ramekin or mug and set next to the cooktop.
4. **For Sauce:** Heat oil in a small frying pan over medium-high heat.
5. Add onion and garlic and sauté until onion is clear and garlic is fragrant (about 5 minutes), stirring constantly.
6. Add tomatoes and spice blend, stir, and cook for 5 minutes.
7. Pour sauce over fish, distributing evenly.
8. Bake fish for 30 minutes or until fish flakes easily when pressed with a finger.
9. Garnish with cashews and cilantro and serve.

FISH TACOS WITH KIMCHI SLAW

Serves 4-6

The instructions for this dish look ridiculously long, but read through them — they are detailed, not complicated. And once you make this dish the first time and get the hang of it, you will want to make it All. The. Time. These tacos are just that good.

Ingredients

Slaw:

- ½ head napa cabbage
- 2 Tbsp. salt
- 14 oz. jar Kimchi, your choice of heat level (2 cups)
- 4 oz. jar diced mild, green chile peppers
- 1 carrot, peeled and grated (½ to 1 cup)
- 4 Tbsp. chopped fresh cilantro

Batter:

- 1 ¼ cup all-purpose flour
- ¼ cup cornstarch
- 1 packet taco seasoning or 3 ½ Tbsp. homemade seasoning from recipe on page 151
- ½ tsp. salt
- ¼ tsp. baking soda
- 2 egg whites (if doubling recipe, use one whole egg + two egg whites)
- 1 cup cold club soda

Fish:

- 2 lb. whitefish fillets (cod, flounder, tilapia, haddock, or other)

Oil:

- 8 cups vegetable oil for deep frying (64 oz.)

Serving:

- 16 oz. package small corn tortillas (24 tortillas, 5 ½" in diameter)
- ½ cup Sriracha mayo (store-bought or homemade: ½ cup mayonnaise + 1 ½ tsp. Sriracha hot chili sauce)

Directions

1. **For Slaw:** Shred cabbage (cut head into quarters, remove core, and cut half of head into thin strips) and layer it in a colander with the salt.
2. Place colander in the sink or over a bowl, and let sit for at least 4 hours for moisture to sweat out of cabbage. If substituting a head of green cabbage, sweating it won't work, and you will need to shred it and cook it before proceeding with this recipe.
3. Squeeze the moisture out of the cabbage, wrap cabbage in a tea towel, and squeeze some more. This should reduce the cabbage to about 1 cup.
4. Transfer cabbage to a medium mixing bowl.
5. Drain the liquid from the kimchi onto the cabbage in the mixing bowl.
6. Finely chop the kimchi and add to the cabbage.
7. Add peppers, carrot, and cilantro to mixture in bowl and stir well.
8. Cover and refrigerate slaw until serving time. Slaw may be made up to a week in advance.
9. **For Batter:** In a small bowl, combine flour, cornstarch, taco seasoning, salt, and baking soda.
10. Mix well with a fork.
11. Add the egg whites and club soda and mix just until blended.
12. **For Frying:** In a stockpot, deep frying pan, electric fryer, or wok, heat oil to 350° (a deep-fry thermometer is invaluable). Oil should be at least 3" deep. Line a baking sheet with several layers of paper towels or newspaper, lay a cooling rack upside down on top of paper, and set aside.
13. Preheat oven to 200°.
14. Wrap tortillas in foil and place in oven to warm.
15. Pat fish dry with a paper towel.
16. If filets are thick (¾" or more), cut them into sticks about 2" x 4". If filets are thin, cut them in half or thirds – a size that will fit in a tortilla.
17. When oil is up to temperature, dip fish pieces into batter, allow excess to drip off, and place battered fish into hot oil. Cook fish in batches, as needed, to avoid over-crowding pan.
18. Cook fish for 4–5 minutes, flipping fish over in the middle of the cooking time.
19. When golden brown on both sides, remove fish from oil using tongs or a kitchen spider, and place on prepared tray to drain.
20. Place tray in oven to stay warm.
21. Allow oil to come back up to 350° before adding next batch of fish.
22. If you have batter left over, it makes delicious onion rings.
23. **To Serve:** Take a warmed tortilla, smear a bit of Sriracha mayo on half of one side, lay one or two pieces of fish on top, and then top them with a generous scoop of slaw.
24. Fold other side of tortilla over to enclose mixture and enjoy!

FISH STICKS
Serves 2-4

After you make these just once, you won't bother with the boxed ones anymore. Seriously. Quick and easy to make, these fish sticks are so flavorful and free of all those unpronounceable ingredients, you will claim these as "your" fish sticks and say bye-bye to the box!

Ingredients

Fish:
- 1 lb. cod, flounder, or haddock filets

Breading:
- 1 egg
- 2 tsp. Worcestershire sauce
- 1 tsp. prepared horseradish
- ½ cup Italian-style bread crumbs
- ¼ cup grated Parmesan cheese
- 1 tsp. onion powder
- ½ tsp. salt

Serving:
- ½ cup of your choice of dipping sauces: tartar sauce (store-bought or homemade from the recipe on page 163), seafood cocktail sauce (store-bought or homemade from the recipe on page 164), and/or ketchup

Directions

1. Preheat oven to 425°.
2. Pat fish dry with a paper towel. Cut the filets crosswise into strips 1" wide.
3. Crack the egg into a shallow bowl. Add the Worcestershire and horseradish. Beat with a fork or whisk until thoroughly blended.
4. In a second shallow bowl, combine the bread crumbs, Parmesan, onion powder, and salt. Mix well.
5. Working with a few fish strips at a time, dip fish into the egg mixture to coat all sides, and then dredge in the bread crumbs, burying or flipping fish sticks to fully coat them.
6. Lay dipped fish sticks on a greased baking sheet.
7. Spray tops of fish sticks with oil or non-stick spray.
8. Bake for 10-15 minutes (until fish sticks flake when touched) flipping fish sticks over in the middle of baking time. Serve with your choice of dipping sauce(s).

MARINATED SALMON

Serves 4

This is an easy, incredibly tasty preparation for salmon. I got the original recipe from my sister-in-law, then messed with it (maybe more than she thought was necessary) to make it my way.

Ingredients

Marinade:

- ¼ cup soy sauce
- 2 Tbsp. brown sugar
- 1 Tbsp. vegetable oil
- 1 Tbsp. rice vinegar
- 2 tsp. grated fresh ginger (peel and grate on a microplane or the finest side of a box grater) or 1 tsp. ground ginger
- 1 tsp. finely minced or pressed garlic (1 large clove)
- ¼ tsp. liquid smoke

Fish:

- 4 salmon steaks or filets (1 ½ to 2 pounds total)

Directions

1. In a one-gallon ziptop bag, mix all marinade ingredients. Close bag and gently slosh it around to blend ingredients.
2. Add fish to bag and gently agitate bag to coat fish in marinade. Remove all air from bag to draw marinade around fish, then seal bag.
3. Allow fish to marinate 1–2 hours, refrigerated.
4. After marinating, cook salmon by baking or grilling.
5. **To Bake:** Preheat oven to 350°. Place fish on a greased baking sheet. Pour a little of the extra marinade on top. Bake fish for 10 minutes per inch of meat thickness.
6. **To Grill:** Transfer fish to greased grill pan or oiled rack of grill. Pour a little of the extra marinade on top. Place fish over medium coals and cook for 10 minutes per inch of meat thickness.
7. When done, the salmon should flake when pressed with a fork or finger, and the inside of the thickest part of the salmon filet should be pink and watery. For best flavor, don't overcook!

SALMON ALFREDO
Serves 4

Certainly for salmon snobs, the use of a pouch of salmon in a recipe is an abomination. But the reality is if you live on a budget and want salmon in your diet, you are going to have to eat it out of a pouch sometimes. This recipe does a magnificent job of transforming this lowly variety into a company-worthy dish. Of course, if you've got salmon jumping into your kitchen straight from the backyard, feel free to upgrade from pouch to fresh. I have included two versions of this dish — one traditional with all the yummy fat in it, and the other a low-fat version for those appalled by heavy cream and butter.

Ingredients

Pasta:
- 8 oz. fettuccine or egg noodles

Traditional Alfredo:
- 3 Tbsp. butter (do not substitute margarine), divided
- 8 oz. package sliced white mushrooms (about 3 cups)
- 2 Tbsp. finely minced white or yellow onion
- 1 cup heavy cream
- 7.1 oz. pouch boneless, skinless pink salmon or two 5 oz. cans boneless, skinless pink salmon, drained
- 1 cup grated Parmesan cheese
- 1 Tbsp. dried parsley

Directions

1. **For Pasta:** Place a 3-quart covered stockpot, half-full of water, over high heat. Add 2 tsp. salt. Make sauce while water heats.
2. **For Sauce:** In a 1-quart saucepan over medium-high heat, melt 1 Tbsp. of the butter and sauté the mushrooms and onion until the onion is translucent, and the mushrooms are cooked (about 5 minutes).
3. Turn heat down to medium and add the rest of the butter and the heavy cream. Stir.
4. Cook until the mixture is hot but not boiling (steam will rise, and tiny bubbles will form around the edge of the cream). Stir often.
5. Add pasta to boiling water and cook according to package instructions.
6. While pasta cooks, add remaining ingredients to sauce. Cook sauce until heated through and thickened slightly.
7. Remove sauce from heat. Serve sauce over individual portions of cooked, drained pasta.

Low-Fat Alfredo:
- 2 Tbsp. butter (margarine, vegetable oil, or olive oil may be substituted)
- 8 oz. package sliced white mushrooms (about 3 cups)
- 2 Tbsp. finely minced white or yellow onion
- 1 Tbsp. flour
- 14 oz. can fat-free evaporated milk (not sweetened, condensed)
- 1 cup grated Parmesan cheese
- 7.1 oz. pouch boneless, skinless pink salmon or two 5 oz. cans boneless, skinless pink salmon, drained
- 1 Tbsp. dried parsley

Directions:

1. **For Pasta:** In a 1-quart saucepan over medium-high heat, melt the butter and sauté the mushrooms and onion until the onion is translucent and the mushrooms are cooked (about 5 minutes).
2. Add the flour and stir until the mushrooms are coated, and no white spots of flour remain.
3. Add the milk, stirring with a whisk to incorporate milk and eliminate lumps.
4. Cook until mixture comes to a boil and thickens slightly. Stir with a spoon almost constantly.
5. While pasta cooks, add remaining ingredients to sauce. Cook sauce until heated through.
6. Remove sauce from heat. Serve sauce over individual portions of cooked, drained pasta.

SALMON CEVICHE
Makes 3 cups

This is an amazing preparation for salmon, but you have to use high quality, wild-caught fish to make it (the fish can be previously frozen but must be from a reputable source). This is because the fish is "cooked" by the acids in the juices.

Ingredients

- 1 lb. high quality, wild caught salmon, cut in small ½" dice
- ⅓ cup lemon juice + lime juice (half-and-half, give-or-take)
- 3 Tbsp. olive oil
- 1 Tbsp. soy sauce
- 1 cup finely diced red onion
- 1 large clove garlic, finely minced or pressed (1 tsp.)
- 1 jalapeño pepper, with seeds, finely minced
- 1 Tbsp. finely minced cilantro (if you hate cilantro, substitute fresh parsley)
- 1 tsp. salt
- ¼ tsp. ground ginger
- ¼ tsp. ground black pepper

Directions

1. In medium mixing bowl, combine all ingredients, gently tossing to coat the fish well.
2. Cover and refrigerate mixture for at least 8 hours before serving.
3. Stir once or twice during this time.
4. Taste and adjust seasonings. Serve chilled or at room temperature.

TUNA-RICE DELIGHT
Serves 3-4

This recipe was adapted and upgraded from my husband's go-to recipe in college: tuna + white rice + Miracle Whip. This more grown-up version is not exactly high-brow, but it does make a tasty, easy, cheap dinner that, in my book, is a cut above a gooey tuna-noodle casserole.

Ingredients

- 1 cup brown rice
- 2 cups vegetable broth (homemade, store-bought, or 2 cups water + 2 tsp. Better Than Bouillon, clam or vegetable flavor)
- two 6 oz. cans water-packed tuna, drained
- ¼ cup mayonnaise
- 1 Tbsp. white balsamic vinegar
- 2 tsp. brown or Dijon-style mustard
- salt and pepper to taste

Directions

1. In 2-quart saucepan, combine rice and broth. Cover, place over medium-high heat, and bring to a boil.
2. Stir, reduce heat to low (2 on a scale of 1 to 10) and cover.
3. Allow rice to cook, undisturbed, for 30 minutes. Turn heat off and allow to sit for 10 minutes more.
4. When rice is cooked and tender, add remaining ingredients. Stir well to combine, then serve.

SALMON QUICHE

Serves 6-8

In the process of writing this cookbook, I asked several trusted friends and relatives to try out some of the recipes, to be sure the instructions were clear, and finished dishes turned out right. Aunt Sallie nabbed this one, exclaiming she hates salmon. I know ... I thought that was strange, too. But I love Aunt Sallie to pieces, and she went on to explain that her husband, Frank, loves salmon, and she is always on the prowl for salmon dishes they might both like. She made this, heavy on the horseradish and without the Tabasco, and called to tell me how happy this quiche made her, declaring the recipe: "Excellent! A keeper!"

Ingredients

Crust:

- 10" deep dish unbaked pie crust (store-bought or homemade from recipe on page 98), optional

Filling:

- 8 oz. package cream cheese, at room temperature
- 1 cup sour cream, plain yogurt, or plain Greek yogurt
- 4 eggs
- 2 Tbsp. all-purpose flour
- 1 tsp. dried dill weed
- 1 tsp. prepared horseradish
- 1 tsp. Tabasco-style hot pepper sauce
- ½ tsp. salt
- ¼ tsp. ground black pepper
- 7.1 oz. pouch skinless, boneless pink salmon or two 5 oz. cans skinless, boneless salmon, drained
- 10 oz. package frozen chopped spinach, thawed and drained
- ½ cup diced red onion or sliced green onions (2-4 onions)
- ½ cup grated Asiago cheese (2 oz.)
- ½ cup grated Parmesan cheese

Directions

1. Prepare crust. If opting to make this quiche crustless, lightly grease a 10" pie plate and set aside.
2. Preheat oven to 375°.
3. In a large mixing bowl, soften cream cheese by pressing and stirring it with a wooden spoon (or make this in a stand mixer with paddle attachment, on low speed).
4. Add the sour cream and stir until mixture is smooth.
5. Add eggs, one at a time, stirring briskly to incorporate thoroughly.
6. Add flour, dill, horseradish, pepper sauce, salt, and pepper. Mix in.
7. Add salmon, spinach, onion, and cheeses and mix well to distribute spinach and to break up any large chunks of salmon.
8. Pour mixture into pie crust or prepared pan.
9. Bake for 45 minutes.
10. Remove from oven and allow to cool for a couple of minutes before slicing into wedges and serving.

Note: Quiche may be made ahead and frozen (after baking). To serve, thaw quiche, cover with aluminum foil, and reheat in a 300° oven for 20-30 minutes.

SPINACH AND FETA STUFFED SALMON

Serves 4

To make this dish the way it is described, you need the "tails" of the salmon steak left on, so you can wrap them around the stuffing. If your fish monger routinely removes these (many do because those strips of salmon flesh cook so much faster than the rest of the steak) then you will need to make this dish in a greased 8" square baking dish. Simply lay the steaks out in the pan, season them, and fill "inside" and in-between the steaks with the stuffing — no need to tie anything up.

Ingredients

Fish:
- four 6 oz. skin-on salmon steaks (not filets), 1" thick (1 ½ lbs. total)
- ¼ tsp. salt
- Pinch ground black pepper

Stuffing:
- 10 oz. package frozen, chopped spinach, thawed and drained
- 4 oz. feta cheese, crumbled (about 1 cup)
- 1 egg
- 1 large clove garlic (1 tsp.), minced and smashed to a paste with ¼ tsp. salt

Assembly:
- 4' baker's twine

Directions

1. Preheat oven to 350°.
2. **For Fish:** On a small, greased baking sheet, lay out salmon steaks. Sprinkle salmon with salt and pepper.
3. **For Stuffing:** In a small mixing bowl, combine ingredients for stuffing. Toss and stir to blend egg in.
4. Divide stuffing into four equal portions. Form each portion into a large ball.
5. Place one ball "inside" each of the salmon steaks, next to the spine. Press stuffing flat to match thickness of salmon.
6. Cut four pieces of baker's twine, each about 12" long. Wrap one piece of twine around the skin side of one salmon steak. Tighten and tie so salmon and stuffing are tight to one another. Repeat tying process with remaining salmon.
7. Bake salmon for 20 minutes. Serve hot.

SWORDFISH KEBABS
Serves 2-4

I don't know why, but I only make these kebabs in the summertime. It might be because of the need to fire up the grill. But, no ... if that's really the reason, then I'm a hypocrite because I brush the snow off and grill other things in the wintertime. It must be how great these taste at an outdoor table on a warm summer evening.

Ingredients

Marinade:

- 2 Tbsp. olive oil
- 2 Tbsp. soy sauce
- 1 Tbsp. fresh lemon juice (⅓ of a lemon)
- 1 Tbsp. grated fresh ginger (peel and grate on a microplane or the finest side of a box grater) or 1 tsp. ground ginger
- 2 large garlic cloves, finely minced or pressed (2 tsp.)
- ¼ tsp. salt
- 1 lb. swordfish steaks, cut into 1" cubes

Kebabs:

- 1 red bell pepper, cut into 1" x 1" pieces
- 1 medium white or yellow onion, outer layers separated and cut into 1" x 1" pieces
- 4 long shish-kebab skewers

Directions

1. **For Marinade:** In a one-gallon ziptop bag, combine marinade ingredients. Close bag and slosh ingredients around to combine.
2. Add cubed fish to marinade. Agitate gently to coat fish.
3. Remove air from bag, seal, and refrigerate for at least 30 minutes and up to 4 hours.
4. If using bamboo skewers, soak them in water while fish marinates.
5. **To Assemble:** Thread cubes of fish and squares of pepper and onion onto the four skewers, beginning and ending with a piece of pepper and a piece of onion. Alternate cubes of fish and squares of veggies, dividing everything as equally as possible between the four skewers.
6. Light a grill, or preheat the broiler, and coat the cooking rack with vegetable oil or nonstick spray.
7. When coals are medium-hot or broiler is up to temperature, lay the shish kebabs on the cooking rack and pour the remaining marinade over top.
8. Leave for 4 minutes and then flip over.
9. Cook 4 minutes more, remove, and serve.

TILAPIA STUFFED WITH LOBSTER

Serves 4-6

This recipe also works well with 6–8 ounces of lump crab meat used in place of the lobster tails. Incredibly delicious either way!

Ingredients

Stuffing:

- 2 cooked lobster tails, diced (if you purchased raw tails, top each with 1 tsp. butter or olive oil, wrap in foil and bake for 15-20 minutes in a 350° oven)
- 2 Tbsp. finely minced white or yellow onion
- 2 eggs
- ½ cup dry bread crumbs
- ¼ tsp. rubbed sage

Fish:

- 2 lbs. tilapia filets (thin filets are needed for this – if your filets are more than ½" thick, cut them in half horizontally)
- ½ tsp. seasoned salt
- ¼ tsp. ground paprika (sweet or hot)

Directions

1. Preheat oven to 350°.
2. In a small mixing bowl, combine ingredients for stuffing.
3. Mix well to distribute eggs throughout mixture.
4. Lay fish fillets out on a greased baking sheet.
5. Divide stuffing evenly between filets, making a mound across the middle of each piece of fish.
6. Fold the two ends of one filet up and over the mound of stuffing and secure with a toothpick.
7. Repeat process with all filets.
8. Sprinkle tops of fish with seasoned salt and paprika.
9. Bake for 20 minutes or until center is firm and fish flakes easily.

Variation:

This dish may also be assembled into a terrine by layering the fish and stuffing into a greased bread pan. Lay half the fish in the bottom of the pan, distributing evenly. Sprinkle half the seasoned salt on top. Top with the stuffing mix, spreading to an even thickness. Top with remaining fish, seasoned salt, and paprika. Bake for 30 minutes (uncovered). Cut in slices and serve.

TUSCAN STUFFED MAHI MAHI

Serves 8

If you ever find yourself hosting a pescatarian Thanksgiving, this is the main dish to make. It is incredibly delicious, with just the right "special occasion" qualities. Even those pesky turkey-lovers around your table with devour this with gusto!

Ingredients

Stuffing:

- 12 oz. package vegetarian bulk sausage
- ½ cup finely minced white or yellow onion
- 1 large clove garlic, finely minced or pressed (1 tsp.)
- 1 egg
- ½ cup dry bread crumbs or cracker crumbs
- ½ tsp. ground savory
- ⅛ tsp. ground black pepper

Fish:

- 8 mahi mahi steaks, each about 1" thick (3 lbs. total)
- 1 Tbsp. olive oil
- 1 tsp. salt
- 1 tsp. paprika (sweet or smoked)
- ¾ cup dry white wine (Sauvignon Blanc or Pinot Grigio)

Sauce:

- Pan drippings
- ½ cup fish stock, clam juice, or water + ½ tsp. Better Than Bouillon Clam Base
- 1 Tbsp. cornstarch

Garnish:

- 2 Tbsp. fresh chives, snipped

Directions

1. **For Stuffing:** Remove veggie protein from packaging and place in medium mixing bowl.
2. Add remaining stuffing ingredients and mix gently with hands until thoroughly combined.
3. Divide mixture into 8 equal portions.
4. **For Fish:** Preheat oven to 350°.
5. With a sharp knife, cut each steak in half horizontally.
6. Open one steak by lifting the upper half, place one portion of stuffing inside, flatten stuffing so it covers fish, and lay the upper half back down over the stuffing.
7. Place stuffed steak in a 9" x 13" baking dish.
8. Repeat stuffing process with other steaks.
9. Brush tops of steaks with olive oil and sprinkle salt and paprika evenly over all.
10. Pour wine into bottom of baking dish, being careful not to rinse the seasoning off the tops of the fish steaks.
11. Bake, uncovered, for 30 minutes.
12. Transfer fish steaks to a serving platter. Cover with aluminum foil to keep warm.
13. **For Sauce:** Combine sauce ingredients in a small saucepan and place over medium-high heat.
14. Cook, stirring constantly, until sauce is bubbly and thickened.
15. Taste, adjust seasonings, and pour sauce over fish.
16. Sprinkle chives over all and serve.

Tuscan Stuffed Mahi Mahi is pictured on page 65

Shrimp Fajitas, recipe on page 92

SHELLFISH ENTREES

Dinner parties are many things to many people, but for me, they are performance art. The host chooses the cast, sets the stage, and then allows the completely improvised script to be written as the night unfolds. I love hosting dinner parties. I love every aspect, but most especially, I love setting the table. Without saying a word, a laid table can convey to my cast of guests what sort of night we will be having, what sort of art we will be creating. Lobster on China? Burgers on divided plates? Candlelight? Chopsticks?

    The same as a theatre troupe collects costumes and props, I collect dishes. I've inherited some, gotten lucky on craigslist for others, and splurged on the rest. I did not always have the means to indulge this passion, so I take an incredible delight in it now.

    I know I am not alone in loving a well-set table. Even for an ordinary weeknight dinner, such a thing conveys welcome, care, and respect. It only takes a few minutes, but I swear it makes the evening more lively and the food more appreciated.

CLAMS IN WHITE SAUCE WITH LINGUINI

Serves 6

I am not a fan of beige food, and this dish is traditionally beige until you add parsley. Trouble is, by the time you add enough parsley to make this entree appetizing, it tastes like my front yard. Which is not as great as it sounds. My solution? Spinach — a companionable, colorful complement to the garlicky goodness of this dish. Oh, and you'll want to wear an apron for this one — the anchovies spatter like crazy as they cook.

Ingredients

Pasta:

- 8 oz. dry linguini noodles

Sauce:

- 2 Tbsp. olive oil
- two 2 oz. tins anchovies packed in oil
- 1 shallot, finely minced (about ¾ cup)
- 9 large cloves finely minced or pressed garlic (3 Tbsp.)
- 2 Tbsp. fresh, minced parsley
- 1 tsp. dried thyme
- ¼ tsp. red pepper flakes
- 1 cup clam juice (nectar drained from clams you will be using, or bottled clam juice)
- ½ cup dry white wine (Sauvignon Blanc or Pinot Grigio)
- 10 oz. package frozen, chopped spinach (thawed but not drained)
- 3 cups cooked or 4 cups fresh, drained, chopped clams (two 16 oz. tubs fresh, two 10 oz. packages frozen, or five 5 oz. cans)
- ½ cup grated fresh Parmesan cheese
- 1 Tbsp. lemon juice
- ½ tsp. salt

Directions

1. **For Pasta:** Place a 4-quart stock pot half-full of water over high heat. Add 2 teaspoons salt, cover, and bring to a boil.
2. **For Sauce:** While water is heating, place a large frying pan over medium heat. When the pan is hot, add the oil, anchovies (with their oil), and shallots. Sauté until the anchovies have melted and the shallots are translucent (about 5 minutes). Stir frequently.
3. Add the garlic, parsley, thyme, and pepper. Stir in.
4. When the garlic is fragrant (less than a minute), add the clam juice, wine and spinach. Stir in.
5. Cook (uncovered) until the liquid has reduced by half and the mixture has thickened a bit (about 10 minutes).
6. Cook pasta until barely al dente while sauce simmers.
7. Drain the cooked pasta and add it, the clams, cheese, lemon juice, and salt to the sauce.
8. Gently stir everything together. Cover and bring sauce back to a simmer.
9. Simmer for 5 minutes, until pasta is tender and raw clams are cooked.
10. Taste, adjust seasonings, and serve.

COCONUT SHRIMP

Serves 6

Most coconut shrimp recipes have you dipping the shrimp in flour, then beaten egg, and finally shredded coconut. While tasty, this method gives the coconut a very tenuous hold on the shrimp, and a lot of the good stuff falls off in the cooking process. My method is different. The shrimp here are coated with a light batter before taking a dip into the coconut, thus giving the coconut a strong hold.

Ingredients

Shrimp:

- 2 lbs. raw jumbo shrimp, peeled and deveined, with tails on (if frozen, thaw)

Batter:

- 1 egg
- ¾ cup unsweetened coconut milk (regular, not lite; ½ of a well-stirred 14 oz. can)
- ½ cup all-purpose flour
- 2 Tbsp. cornstarch
- ½ tsp. onion powder
- ¼ tsp. salt

Breading:

- 14 oz. bag sweetened, flaked coconut (4 cups; if substituting unsweetened coconut, add 2 Tbsp. granulated sugar to coconut and toss to coat)

Oil:

- 8 cups coconut or vegetable oil for deep frying (64 oz.)

Directions

1. **For Shrimp:** Lay shrimp out on paper towels and pat completely dry. Shrimp must be dry for batter to stick.
2. **For Batter:** In a small mixing bowl, combine egg and milk. Beat briskly with a fork or whisk.
3. Add remaining ingredients for batter and stir just until combined.
4. **For Breading:** Dump coconut in a shallow bowl or pan.
5. **For Frying:** In a stockpot, deep frying pan, electric fryer, or wok, heat oil to 375° (a deep-fry thermometer is invaluable). Oil should be at least 3" deep. Line a baking sheet with several layers of paper towels or newspaper, lay a cooling rack upside down on top of paper, and set aside.
6. When oil is up to temperature, hold each shrimp by the tail, dip it into the batter, and allow the excess batter to drip off.
7. Dredge battered shrimp in coconut flakes.
8. Drop shrimp into hot oil. Quickly repeat dipping and dredging process with additional shrimp. Do not over-crowd oil. Fry shrimp in batches, as needed.
9. Cook each batch of shrimp for 3–5 minutes (depending on size of shrimp) flipping shrimp over in the middle of cooking time.
10. Remove cooked shrimp from oil with a strainer or kitchen spider and place on prepared baking sheet to drain.
11. Allow cooking oil to get back up to temperature before adding next batch of shrimp.

Shellfish Entrees

COCONUT-LIME SHRIMP
Serves 2-3

This is a quick, delicious dish that makes a great meal if paired with a green vegetable or salad, and a cut-up fresh pineapple.

Ingredients

Shrimp:
- 1 lb. raw shrimp, peeled and deveined

Sauce:
- ½ cup coconut milk (⅓ of a well-stirred 14 oz. can)
- 6 Tbsp. unsweetened shredded coconut (if substituting sweetened, omit sugar and add a dash more lime juice)
- 2 Tbsp. olive oil
- 2 Tbsp. fresh lime juice (1 lime)
- ½ tsp. fresh lime zest
- 1 tsp. onion powder
- ½ tsp. granulated sugar
- ½ tsp. salt
- pinch of chili powder
- dash of Tabasco-style hot pepper sauce
- 1 tsp. cornstarch
- 1 tsp. water

Rice:
- 1 cup brown rice
- 2 cups vegetable broth or water

Directions

1. In a medium mixing bowl, combine all sauce ingredients except cornstarch and water. Stir vigorously with a fork.
2. Add shrimp and stir gently to coat shrimp in sauce. Allow to sit while rice cooks.
3. In a rice cooker or on the stovetop, cook rice according to the package instructions.
4. When rice is about 15 minutes from being done, heat a large frying pan over medium-high heat.
5. Dump the shrimp and sauce into the hot pan and spread shrimp out to cover the pan in an even layer.
6. As the shrimps turn pink and opaque on the bottom, flip them over one by one (this takes about 3 minutes).
7. When shrimps are pink and opaque on the second side, and are firm to the touch, remove them to a serving bowl.
8. Continue in this manner until all shrimp are cooked and removed from the frying pan. Depending on the size of your shrimp and your frying pan, this will take 5-10 minutes total.
9. Mix cornstarch and water together to form a paste and add to remaining sauce in frying pan. Stir continuously and cook until sauce is thickened (less than 1 minute).
10. Pour sauce over shrimp. Serve shrimp and sauce over cooked rice.

CRAB EGG ROLLS

Makes 10-15 egg rolls (depending on size of cabbage)

My biggest complaint about restaurant egg rolls — aside from the fact that even the seafood ones contain pork — is they are full of "filler" vegetables and hardly any good stuff. Not these. Chocked full of crab, with vegetables in a supporting role, these are outstanding!

Ingredients

Filling:

- 1 head napa cabbage
- 3 Tbsp. salt
- 2 Tbsp. cornstarch
- 8 oz. lump crabmeat or three 6 oz. cans lump crab, drained
- 1 bunch green onions, thinly sliced (2 cups)
- 4 tsp. soy sauce
- 1 tsp. sesame oil

Wrappers:

- 16 oz. package egg roll wrappers (24 wrappers in package)

Oil:

- 8 cups vegetable oil for deep frying (64 oz.)

Serving:

- ½ cup sweet-and-sour sauce (store bought or from a recipe on page 162)

Directions

1. **For Filling:** Shred cabbage and layer it in a colander with the salt.
2. Place colander in the sink or over a bowl, and let sit for at least 4 hours, for moisture to sweat out of cabbage. If substituting a head of green cabbage, sweating it won't work, and you will need to shred it and cook it before proceeding with this recipe.
3. Once cabbage is fully sweated, squeeze the moisture out of it. Wrap the cabbage in a clean tea towel, and squeeze some more (you should end up with 2–3 cups cabbage).
4. Transfer cabbage to a medium mixing bowl and sprinkle cornstarch on top.
5. Mix until no white powder remains.
6. Add crab, onions, soy sauce, and sesame oil to cabbage. Stir until well mixed.
7. **For Frying:** In a stockpot, deep frying pan, electric fryer, or wok, heat oil to 350° (a deep-fry thermometer is invaluable). Oil should be at least 3" deep. Line a baking sheet with several layers of paper towels or newspaper, lay a cooling rack upside down on top of paper, and set aside.
8. Lay out an egg roll wrapper and mound ¼ cup filling mixture in the center.
9. Fold and seal according to wrapper package directions, moistening the edge of the wrapper with water, then folding one corner over filling, followed by two side corners, then rolling tightly towards the fourth corner.
10. Repeat with remaining wrappers and filling.
11. When oil is ready, fry egg rolls 4 or 5 at a time, to avoid overcrowding pan.
12. Fry each batch for 5 minutes, turning egg rolls over in the middle of cooking.
13. Remove egg rolls from oil with a strainer or kitchen spider and place on prepared tray to drain. Allow oil to come back to 350° before adding next batch of egg rolls.
14. Serve egg rolls hot, with sweet-and-sour sauce on the side for dipping. Accompany egg rolls with edamame (raw soybeans, steamed) and a steamed vegetable for a complete meal.

CRAB QUICHE
Serves 4-6

This is like a savory cheesecake — rich and very, very satisfying. Canned crab is cheaper but harsher and less sweet than real crab legs or lump crab meat. In this recipe, using both types of crab balances out the flavors while keeping costs in check.

Ingredients

Crust:

- 9" deep dish unbaked pie crust (store-bought or homemade from recipe on page 98), optional

Filling:

- 8 oz. package cream cheese, room temperature
- ½ cup sour cream, plain yogurt, or plain Greek yogurt
- 3 eggs
- ½ tsp. seasoned salt
- ½ tsp. Tabasco-style hot pepper sauce
- 6 oz. can crabmeat (any variety), drained
- 8 oz. lump crabmeat (8 oz. imitation crab, diced, may be substituted)
- 1 cup grated cheese (4 oz.), preferably swiss, provolone, Jarlsberg, or gouda
- 2 green onions, thinly sliced (about ½ cup)

Directions

1. Prepare crust. If opting to make this quiche crustless, lightly grease a 9" pie plate and set aside.
2. Preheat oven to 425°.
3. In a large mixing bowl, soften the cream cheese by pressing and stirring it with the back of a wooden spoon.
4. Add the sour cream and stir until the mixture is smooth.
5. Add eggs, one at a time, stirring briskly to incorporate thoroughly.
6. Add salt and Tabasco and blend in.
7. Add remaining ingredients and mix gently just until combined. Pour mixture into pie crust or prepared pan.
8. Bake for 15 minutes.
9. Turn oven temperature down to 350° and continue baking for 30 additional minutes.
10. Remove from oven and allow to cool for a couple of minutes before slicing into wedges and serving.
11. Quiche may be made ahead and frozen (after baking). Thaw quiche, cover with aluminum foil, and reheat in a 300° oven for 20–30 minutes.

FRIED OYSTERS

Serves 2-4

For most of my life, I wondered why anyone would voluntarily eat oysters. They are expensive, and they look like boogers. Turns out, people eat them because they are delicious. And in a cooked state, they taste a bit like clams, which makes them positively divine when battered and fried.

Ingredients

Oysters:

- 1 lb. shucked oysters, drained (no need to pat them dry)

Breading:

- ½ cup buttermilk
- 1 cup whole wheat pastry flour
- ½ cup all-purpose flour
- ½ cup cornmeal
- 1 Tbsp. granulated sugar
- 1 Tbsp. Old Bay Seasoning

Frying:

- 8 cups vegetable oil for deep-frying (64 oz.)

Serving:

- ½ cup tartar sauce (store-bought or homemade from recipe on page 163)
- ½ cup seafood cocktail sauce (store-bought or homemade from recipe on page 164)
- 4 sub-style Italian rolls (optional)

Directions

1. **For Frying:** In a stockpot, deep frying pan, electric fryer, or wok, heat oil to 375° (a deep-fry thermometer is invaluable). Oil should be at least 3" deep. Line a baking sheet with several layers of paper towels or newspaper, lay a cooling rack upside down on top of paper, and set aside.
2. **For Breading:** In a small mixing bowl, combine oysters and buttermilk. Gently stir. Let sit for 5 minutes.
3. In a one gallon ziptop bag, combine dry ingredients for breading. Shake to mix.
4. When oil is up to temperature, remove two handfuls of oysters from the bowl (about half). Drop the oysters into the bag of breading. Seal bag and shake to coat oysters.
5. Remove breaded oysters from bag and drop them into the hot oil.
6. Fry the oysters for 2-3 minutes, flipping them over in the middle of the cooking time. When done, oysters will be golden brown and crisp.
7. Remove the oysters from the oil with tongs or a kitchen spider and lay them out on the prepared tray to drain. Allow the oil to come back up to temperature before repeating the process for the remaining oysters.
8. Serve oysters hot with tartar sauce and cocktail sauce on the side for dipping. Fried Oysters may be made into po' boy sandwiches by stuffing the oysters into Italian rolls spread with tartar sauce.

LOBSTER MAC-N-CHEESE

Makes 9" x 13" pan; serves 6

After our move to the East Coast, I was excited to find lobster mac-'n-cheese on the menu of a local restaurant. I ordered some and was underwhelmed by the dish that arrived. I thought I could do better. It took several tries and additional tweaking, but now I have.

Ingredients

Pasta:

- 1 lb. whole wheat elbow macaroni
- 1 cup heavy cream

Cheese Sauce:

- 3 Tbsp. butter
- 3 Tbsp. all-purpose flour
- ½ tsp. dried mustard
- 3 cups fish stock (or 1 ½ cups bottled clam juice + 1 ½ cups water)
- ½ cup heavy cream
- 8 oz. gouda cheese, grated or diced
- 8 oz. bag 6-cheese Italian blend grated cheese

Seafood and Broccoli:

- 7 oz. container cooked lobster meat, thawed and drained
- 6 oz. can lump crab meat, drained
- 1 head broccoli, cut into florets (peel and dice main stem), cooked to tender-crisp

Topping:

- 1 cup bread crumbs
- 1 cup grated Parmesan cheese

Directions

1. **For Pasta:** In large stock pot, bring 2 quarts water + 2 tsp. salt to boil and cook pasta until al dente, according to package directions.
2. Drain pasta and return to pot with 1 cup cream (omit cream if using white pasta). Stir.
3. Cover pasta until sauce is ready.
4. Start cheese sauce right after you put the pasta water on to boil.
5. **For Cheese Sauce:** In 2-quart saucepan, melt butter over medium heat.
6. Add flour and mustard to make a roux. Stir constantly and cook for a full minute to cook out raw flavor of flour.
7. Add fish stock and cream to roux. Stir with a whisk until smooth.
8. Bring mixture to a gentle boil and boil a few minutes, until thickened. Stir frequently.
9. Reduce heat to low. Add cheeses, stirring well to incorporate. Cook just until cheese is melted.
10. Remove sauce from heat and preheat oven to 350°.
11. **To Assemble:** Add lobster, crab, and broccoli to cooked, drained pasta in pot.
12. Pour cheese sauce over top of everything. Stir gently to combine all ingredients.
13. Transfer mixture to a 9" x 13" casserole dish or baking pan.
14. Mix bread crumbs and Parmesan cheese together for topping. Sprinkle mixture over top of all.
15. Mac-'n-cheese may be made to this point ahead of time, covered, and refrigerated – up to a few days – or frozen (thaw before baking).
16. Bake for 30 minutes and serve.

Eat Meat Without Feet

MUSSELS

Serves 2

Mussels are cheap and tasty, and this recipe is quick and good. Some, but not all, of the mussels will fall out of their shells during cooking. Remove any empty shells before serving, but ladle the rest — shells and all — over the noodles. This presentation is beautiful, and each person can either suck the little nuggets of meat out of their shells, or scoop them out with a spoon and drop them into the noodles and broth. Be sure to provide an empty bowl in the middle of the table for the discarded shells.

Ingredients

Mussels:
- 3 lbs. mussels, fresh in their shells
- ¼ cup flour

Sauce:
- 1 Tbsp. olive oil
- 1 Tbsp. butter
- 2 Tbsp. minced fresh garlic (6 large cloves)
- ¼ cup diced red bell pepper (about ¼ of a large pepper)
- 1 bunch scallions, sliced thin (about 1 ½ cups)
- 1 Tbsp. minced fresh or dried parsley
- 14 oz. can diced tomatoes (2 cups)
- 2 tsp. soy sauce
- ½ cup dry white wine (Sauvignon Blanc or Pinot Grigio)
- ½ cup bottled clam juice or fish stock

Pasta:
- 8 oz. whole grain egg noodles

Directions

1. Before cooking, discard any mussels that are open.
2. Remove and discard all beards (hairy bits sticking out of the shells) and scrub the shells if they seem dirty. Farmed mussels generally don't require scrubbing.
3. Soak the mussels for 30 minutes in a large bowl of cool water (+/- 2 quarts) with the flour added to it. This will get the mussels to release any sand they are harboring.
4. After soaking, rinse and drain mussels.
5. **For Pasta:** For the noodles to be done at the same time as the mussels, start heating a pot of water for the noodles about 10 minutes before beginning to cook the mussels.
7. **For Mussels:** In a stock pot large enough to accommodate all the mussels, heat the olive oil and butter over medium-high heat.
8. When the butter is melted, add the garlic and red pepper and sauté for about 30 seconds.
9. Add the scallions, parsley, tomatoes, soy sauce, wine, and clam juice. Cover and bring to a boil.
10. Add the mussels and cover. Cook for 10 minutes, stirring once in the middle of cooking.
11. Add the noodles to the pot of boiling water and cook according to package instructions.
12. Check mussels after cooking and remove and discard any that are not open.
13. **To Serve:** Drain the noodles and divide them evenly between two individual serving bowls (big enough to hold 3-4 cups each).
14. Divide the mussels and broth in half, ladling each portion over the noodles.

SCALLOPS AND GNOCCHI IN CREAM SAUCE

Serves 4

After you make this dish and get the hang of it, you will easily make it in under 30 minutes. Rich, scrumptious, and fit for royalty, this is one of those recipes that merits memorizing.

Ingredients

Pasta:

- 2 quarts water for cooking + 2 tsp. salt
- 16 oz. package potato gnocchi (whole wheat or white)

Sauce:

- 2 Tbsp. butter
- 1 shallot, finely minced, or ⅓ cup finely minced white or yellow onion
- 1 tsp. finely minced or pressed garlic (1 large clove)
- ½ cup dry white wine (Sauvignon Blanc or Pinot Grigio)
- 1 cup heavy cream
- 1 tsp. Better Than Bouillon Clam Base
- 1 Tbsp. dried parsley

Scallops:

- 2 Tbsp. olive or vegetable oil
- 1 ½ lbs. sea scallops, rubbery "beards" removed
- ⅛ tsp. salt

Garnish:

- ½ cup grated Parmesan cheese

Directions

1. **For Pasta:** Heat water and salt in a covered 3-quart pot over high heat.
2. **For Sauce:** While water is heating, make sauce. In a 1-quart saucepan over medium heat, melt butter.
3. Add the shallot and garlic. Sauté for 2 minutes, stirring constantly.
4. Add wine and cook until liquid is reduced by half (5–10 minutes).
5.
6. Add remaining ingredients for sauce. Stir to dissolve bouillon.
7. Bring sauce up to a simmer (bubbles will form around the edges of the mixture) then reduce heat to the lowest setting possible.
8. Allow sauce to gently simmer and thicken while you prepare the scallops and gnocchi. Stir sauce occasionally.
9. **For Scallops:** Place a large frying pan over medium-high heat (6 on a scale of 1 to 10). Add oil.
10. When oil is hot, place scallops in pan. Lightly sprinkle salt over all.
11. Cook scallops until they turn opaque halfway up their sides (about 3 minutes). Flip scallops over and cook until they are opaque all the way through and firm to the touch (another 3 minutes or so).
12. Remove scallops from heat.
13. **For Pasta:** After you flip the scallops over, add the gnocchi and salt to the pot of boiling water.
14. Cook gnocchi until they float to the surface (about 2 minutes). Remove gnocchi with a slotted spoon or strainer as they are done and transfer them to a platter or 2-quart serving bowl.
15. Top the gnocchi with the cooked scallops and pour the cream sauce over all. Garnish with a sprinkling of Parmesan cheese.

SEAFOOD NEWBURG

Serves 12

This is another "special occasion" dish because it takes more time to make than a normal human has to spare during the workweek, and it is pricier than everyday dishes. When you make it, expect to feel like you fussed, and expect your guests to talk about this incredible dish for days afterward.

Ingredients

Rice:
- 4 cups brown rice
- 8 cups vegetable broth or water

Sauce:
- 8 Tbsp. butter (1 stick)
- 1 medium white or yellow onion, finely minced (about 1 cup)
- 24 oz. package mushrooms, sliced (about 8 cups)
- ½ cup all-purpose flour
- 4 cups fish stock (or 2 cups bottled clam juice + 2 cups water)
- 2 cups heavy cream
- 1 ½ tsp. paprika
- pinch cayenne pepper
- 4 egg yolks
- ⅓ cup dry white wine (Sauvignon Blanc or Pinot Grigio)
- 1 tsp. dry mustard
- 1 tsp. salt
- ¼ tsp. black pepper

Seafood:
- 1 lb. lobster meat or lump crabmeat, coarsely chopped (imitation crab may be substituted in a pinch)
- 2 lbs. uncooked shrimp, peeled and deveined
- 1 lb. sea scallops, tough "beards" removed

Directions

1. **For Rice:** In a rice cooker or on the stovetop, cook rice according to the package instructions. While rice is cooking, prepare the sauce.
2. **For Sauce:** In a 3-quart stock pot, melt butter over medium-high heat and sauté onions and mushrooms until onions are transparent. The mushrooms will not be fully cooked.
3. Add flour and stir until mushrooms are coated and no white spots of flour remain.
4. Cook one more minute, stirring constantly, and then add the fish stock.
5. Stir with a whisk and bring to a boil, stirring often.
6. Once boiling, stir almost constantly and cook until sauce has thickened (about 2 minutes).
7. Reduce heat to low.
8. Add cream, paprika, and cayenne. Stir and cover.
9. In a medium mixing bowl, combine the egg yolks, wine, mustard, salt, and pepper. Beat with a whisk until the yolks turn slightly pale.
10. When the sauce in the large pot has reached a simmer, remove 1 cup of it.
11. Working quickly, add the cup of hot sauce to the egg yolk mixture, 1 large spoonful at a time, mixing vigorously with a whisk after each addition. If done properly, the yolk mixture will be smooth, pudding-like, and warm; if done improperly, the yolk mixture will be disgusting, lumpy, and unsalvageable. Do this step again, if necessary, to get it right.
12. When all the sauce has been incorporated into the yolks properly, add the yolk mixture to the large pot and stir well. Cover.
13. Bring sauce to a simmer but do not allow it to reach a full boil.
14. Add lobster, shrimp, and scallops to the simmering sauce. Stir gently and cover.
15. Cook for about 10 minutes, stirring occasionally. When done, the shrimp and scallops will be opaque and the sauce will be hot (tiny bubbles will form around the edge of the pan) but not boiling.
16. Taste the sauce, add salt and pepper as needed. Serve immediately by ladling sauce over individual portions of hot, cooked rice.

SEAFOOD LASAGNA

Makes a 3" high lasagna in a 9" x 13" pan; serves 12

Very rich and decadent — perfect for a holiday celebration or other special occasion. After concocting this recipe and making it a couple times for our family to try and tweak, I made this "for real" for a Christmas party at my husband's work. Several years later, I made it for a Christmas gathering with extended family, and ultimately, I made it for a fancy-pants, sit-down dinner party my husband and I hosted for our joint 50th birthday parties. In all cases, people about lost their minds over how incredible this lasagna was, couldn't believe I made it myself from my own recipe, and raved all night long about "that" lasagna.

Ingredients

Alfredo Layer:

- 6 Tbsp. butter
- ½ cup finely minced white or yellow onion
- 2 cups heavy cream
- 1 cup grated Parmesan cheese
- 1 lb. crabmeat (lump or imitation), cut into small chunks
- 1 ½ lbs. uncooked shrimp, shelled and de-veined (any size will work, but smaller is better)
- 2 Tbsp. dried parsley

Mushroom Layer:

- 6 Tbsp. butter, divided
- 3 lbs. sliced mushrooms (any kind or a mix of kinds; 18 cups)
- 1 cup finely diced white or yellow onion (1 medium onion)
- 2 Tbsp. fresh lemon juice (½ of a large lemon)
- ½ cup Worcestershire sauce
- 2 tsp. Tabasco-style hot pepper sauce
- 1 tsp. salt
- ¼ tsp. black pepper
- 1 Tbsp. dry white wine (Sauvignon Blanc or Pinot Grigio)

Cheese:

- 1 ½ lbs. grated mozzarella cheese
- ¼ cup grated Parmesan cheese

Pasta:

- 15 lasagna noodles

Directions

1. **For Alfredo Layer:** In a 3-quart saucepan over medium heat, melt butter and sauté onions until they are translucent.
2. Add heavy cream and heat to a simmer, stirring almost constantly (steam will rise and tiny bubbles will form around edge of pan).
3. Add remaining ingredients and allow sauce to remain on the heat for 5 minutes, until shrimps are cooked – they will turn opaque and feel firm to the touch.
4. Remove from heat and set aside.
5. While preparing mushroom layer, cook lasagna noodles until al dente, according to package instructions. Drain.
6. **For Mushroom Layer:** In a large frying pan over medium-high heat, melt 4 tablespoons of butter. Sauté mushrooms and onions until mushrooms are cooked and onions are translucent. If you don't have a frying pan large enough to cook it all at once, cook the mushroom-onion mixture in two batches and then recombine them (the mushrooms will cook down a lot).
7. Add lemon juice, Worcestershire, Tabasco, salt, and pepper to mushroom mixture.
8. Cook until liquid is reduced by half.
9. Add wine and remaining 2 Tbsp. butter to thicken. Stir constantly.
10. When butter has melted and is fully incorporated, remove mushroom mixture from heat and set aside.
11. **To Assemble Lasagna:** Preheat oven to 375°.
12. In the bottom of a deep 9" x 13" baking pan, spread 1 cup of the Alfredo sauce.
13. Top with 3 lasagna noodles, laid out next to each other.
14. Top noodles with half the remaining Alfredo sauce, spread to an even thickness.
15. Top this with two handfuls of shredded mozzarella cheese and then 3 more noodles.
16. Top this with half the mushroom mixture, spread to an even thickness, and 3 more noodles.
17. Top this with the remaining Alfredo sauce and two handfuls of shredded mozzarella.
18. Lay on 3 more noodles and the remaining mushroom mixture.
19. Top this with the last 3 noodles.
20. Sprinkle the remaining mozzarella and Parmesan cheeses on top.
21. Bake lasagna for 30–45 minutes, until cheese on top is browned and knife or pick inserted into center of pan comes out hot.
22. Allow to sit for 5 minutes before cutting into squares and serving.

SHRIMP FAJITAS

Serves 2-4

Oh, man ... these are so good. Make them once, and I swear, you won't pay restaurant prices for them ever again.

Ingredients

Shrimp:

- 1 lb. raw, peeled (tail-off), de-veined shrimp (any size)
- ½ jalapeño pepper, seeded and finely minced (leave seeds in for spicy fajitas)
- 2 tsp. finely minced or pressed garlic (2 large cloves) or ½ tsp. garlic powder
- 1 tsp. chili powder
- 1 tsp. paprika (sweet, not hot)
- 1 tsp. granulated sugar
- ½ tsp. dried oregano
- ½ tsp. salt
- ¼ tsp. ground coriander
- ¼ tsp. ground celery seed
- ¼ tsp. ground black pepper
- ⅛ tsp. ground cardamom
- ⅛ tsp. ground cumin
- ⅛ tsp. ground turmeric
- ⅛ tsp. ground marjoram
- 2 Tbsp. fresh lime juice (1 lime)

Vegetables:

- 2 Tbsp. vegetable oil
- 1 large white or yellow onion, trimmed and cut top to bottom in thin wedges (about 2 cups)
- 2 bell peppers (green, red, yellow, orange, or any combination), seeded and cut top to bottom in ¼" wide strips (about 3 cups)

Directions

1. In a small, non-reactive mixing bowl (no aluminum), combine shrimp ingredients.
2. Stir gently until shrimp are coated. Set aside while you prepare and cook vegetables.
3. In a large frying pan over medium heat, place oil. When oil is hot, add onions and peppers. Sauté, stirring often, until onions are translucent and just beginning to brown (about 10 minutes).
4. Move vegetables to one side of the pan.
5. Add shrimp and marinade to the other side of the pan. Cook, stirring and flipping shrimp over as needed, until shrimp are opaque, firm, and cooked through.
6. Stir vegetables once or twice while shrimp are cooking.
7. When shrimp are cooked through, stir vegetables and shrimp together in pan.
8. Remove pan from heat. Squeeze or sprinkle fresh lime juice over shrimp-vegetable mixture. Stir lime juice into mixture.
9. Spoon fajita filling into tortillas and top with dollops of sour cream. Fold or roll up tortilla around filling.

Serving:

- 2 Tbsp. fresh lime juice (1 lime)
- 4 whole wheat tortillas, warmed
- ½ cup sour cream

Shrimp Fajitas are pictured on page 79

Taco Casserole, recipe on page 112

VEGETARIAN ENTREES

My exposure to vegetarian fare — aside from cheese pizza and boxed mac-'n-cheese — began in college. It was there I learned vegetarians ate more than salad (my mother's rabbit-centric view), and I often chose the vegetarian entree in the cafeteria. Then, I spent the fall semester of my senior year in Philadelphia, completing an internship. I lived in an apartment with four other women, and we agreed to take turns in the kitchen, each cooking dinner one night a week. We lived on meager budgets, and one of the women was a vegetarian, so we avoided meat as much as possible.

The five of us were at all levels of cooking proficiency, from the young woman who was apprenticing with a Michelin-star chef, to the young woman who struggled (Every. Friday. Night.) to make pancakes from a mix. I fell in the middle of the pack. I knew things but not that many things.

Trips to the large, boisterous Italian Market every Saturday were a blur of firsts for me: first time I visited a spice shop; first time I saw rabbit carcasses in a meat case; first time I entered a cheese store (and stepped into nirvana); first time I saw cookware being made; and the first time I saw an entire stall full of dried hot peppers in every size, shape, and color. That market was inspiration personified to me. And one Saturday … I bought falafel mix from the market, pitas from the Lebanese market we lived above, and I made something entirely new (to me) for dinner.

BIBIMBAP
Serves 4

Bibimbap is considered the national dish of Korea and is traditionally made with beef. Here is my vegetarian version of this incredible dish, featuring crispy tofu. There are a lot of separate elements to Bibimbap, so this is not a quick weeknight throw-together meal. But on a weekend when you have time, or a date night when you want to impress, this is the thing to make. The separate elements create a colorful, spectacular presentation, and the combination of flavors is positively unforgettable.

--- Ingredients ---

Sauce:
Makes 8 servings

- 1 ripe Asian pear or Bosc pear, peeled, cored, and grated (capture all juices)
- ¼ cup very finely minced red onion or Vidalia onion
- ¼ cup soy sauce
- 2 Tbsp. brown sugar
- 2 – 3 Tbsp. gochujang (Korean fermented hot red pepper paste)
- 2 Tbsp. toasted sesame oil
- 1 Tbsp. rice wine vinegar
- 1 Tbsp. minced garlic, smashed to a paste with a pinch of salt (3 large cloves)
- 1 Tbsp. grated fresh ginger (peel and grate on a microplane or the finest side of a box grater) or 1 tsp. ground ginger

Rice:
- 1 cup brown rice
- 2 cups vegetable broth or water

Proteins:
- 14 oz. package extra-firm tofu, drained
- 1 Tbsp. soy sauce or tamari
- 1 Tbsp. sesame oil
- 1 Tbsp. cornstarch
- 2 Tbsp. butter or vegetable oil
- 4 large eggs

Vegetables:
- 3 Tbsp. vegetable oil

- 8 oz. package sliced shiitake or white mushrooms + 1 Tbsp. sesame oil + ½ tsp. salt

- 1 cup carrots cut in matchstick julienne or grated lengthwise + 1 Tbsp. toasted sesame oil + ¼ tsp. salt

- 10 oz. package frozen leaf spinach, thawed (do not drain) + 1 Tbsp. minced garlic (3 large cloves) smashed to a paste with ½ tsp. salt

- 8 oz. fresh mung bean sprouts or 14 oz. can mung bean sprouts, drained + 1 Tbsp. rice wine vinegar + 1 Tbsp. toasted sesame oil + ¼ tsp. salt

Directions

1. **For Sauce:** In a small mixing bowl, combine all ingredients for sauce. Stir vigorously with a whisk. Set aside. (Sauce may be made up to 3 days ahead of time, covered, and refrigerated.)
2. **For Rice:** Cook rice on stovetop or in a rice cooker, according to package directions. Prepare rest of dish while rice is cooking.
3. **For Tofu:** Cut the block of tofu horizontally into 3 slabs. Lay slabs out flat between several layers of paper towels or a folded tea towel. Weigh down tofu. Let sit at least 10 minutes to press excess moisture out.
4. Preheat oven to 400°.
5. Line a small baking sheet with non-stick silicone or a piece of kitchen parchment.
6. Cut each slab of tofu into 9 pieces. Transfer pieces to a small mixing bowl. Add soy sauce and oil and toss gently to coat tofu.
7. Add cornstarch and toss until tofu is coated and no white spots of cornstarch remain. (Do not add the soy sauce, oil, and cornstarch all at once.)
8. Transfer tofu to baking sheet, laying the cubes out flat in a single layer.
9. Bake tofu for 30 minutes, flipping pieces over in the middle of baking time.
10. **For Vegetables:** Line up four small mixing bowls and place each vegetable with its accompanying ingredients in one of the bowls. Stir each concoction to combine.
11. Place a large frying pan over medium heat. When the pan is hot, add 1 Tbsp. vegetable oil and swirl to coat. Add the mushroom mixture and sauté until mushrooms are just cooked. Return mushrooms to their bowl.
12. Return frying pan to burner. Sauté each of the remaining vegetables separately in a bit of vegetable oil for about 3 minutes each until heated through. When hot, return each vegetable to its bowl.

13. In the same frying pan, heat the butter for frying the eggs. When the butter is melted, crack the four eggs into the pan (north-south-east-west) keeping them separate. Cover the pan. Cook the eggs until sunny-side-up (whites fully cooked, yolks still runny). Remove pan from heat.
14. **To Serve:** Divide rice between four large, individual serving bowls – ¾ cup rice per bowl.
15. Around the edge of the bowl, top the rice with piles of vegetables. Keep the piles separate, and divide the vegetables evenly between the four bowls.
16. In the center, place the cubes of tofu, dividing evenly. Drizzle 3 Tbsp. sauce over each bowl.
17. Top each bowl with a sunny-side-up fried egg. Serve.
18. To eat, break the yolk of the egg, stir everything together, and dig in!

BISCUITS AND SAUSAGE GRAVY

Serves 4-6

This is technically a breakfast dish, but I must confess, I never make it for breakfast, as I am not the sort of person to roll out of bed at 6 a.m., ready to cook up a storm. Hearty, meaty, and delicious, I make this for dinner instead, although leftovers are often enjoyed for breakfast the next day. The biscuit recipe featured here comes from Sara Moulton, former editor of Gourmet Magazine, and is a favorite of mine for its ease and for the tenderness of the finished biscuits.

Ingredients

Barley:
- ½ cup pearl barley
- 1 cup water

Biscuits:
- 1 cup all-purpose flour
- 1 cup whole wheat pastry flour
- 2 Tbsp. raw or granulated sugar
- 1 Tbsp. baking powder
- ½ tsp. salt
- 1 ¼ cups heavy cream

Gravy:
- 2 Tbsp. olive or vegetable oil
- 12 oz. package vegetarian bulk sausage
- 1 green bell pepper, diced (about 1 ½ cups) or 8 oz. package sliced mushrooms (any variety, about 3 cups)
- 2 Tbsp. all-purpose flour
- ½ tsp. ground black pepper
- 2 cups vegetable broth (store-bought, homemade, or 2 cups water + 2 tsp. Better Than Bouillon vegetable or vegetarian chicken flavor)
- 1 cup heavy cream

Directions

1. **For Barley:** In 1-quart saucepan, combine pearl barley and water and place over medium-high heat. Cover and bring to a boil.
2. Reduce heat to low and simmer for 20 minutes.
3. Turn heat off but leave barley on warm burner to finish cooking. Prepare biscuits while barley is cooking.
4. **For Biscuits:** Preheat oven to 425°.
5. In a large mixing bowl, combine all dry ingredients.
6. Add heavy cream and gently mix in using hands. Mix only until a dough forms, or the biscuits will be tough from over-kneading. If dry flour remains at the bottom of the bowl, add a bit more cream to moisten.
7. To shape the biscuits, the dough may be dropped by large spoonfuls onto a baking sheet (recipe should make 12 biscuits) or may be rolled out and cut.
8. To roll out, sprinkle flour on a work surface and place dough on top. Sprinkle top of dough lightly with flour and use a rolling pin to roll the dough to ¾" thick. Cut with round cookie cutter or glass and place on ungreased baking sheet, spacing about 1" apart. Don't twist the cutter as you work. A twisting motion will seal the edges of the biscuits and render them unable to rise properly. Reroll scraps of dough and cut.
9. Bake biscuits for 15 minutes.
10. **For Gravy:** While biscuits are baking, make gravy. Place a large frying pan over medium-high heat.
11. When pan is warm, add oil, veggie sausage, and peppers (or mushrooms).
12. Sauté, breaking up any large chunks of sausage as the mixture cooks. Stir frequently.
13. When sausage is crumbly and peppers are soft (about 10 minutes), add flour and black pepper and stir until no white spots of flour remain.
14. Add broth and stir, scraping the bottom of the pan to loosen all the browned bits.
15. Bring mixture to a soft boil and cook a few minutes until thickened. Stir almost constantly.
16. Add heavy cream, heat through, and serve.
17. To serve, place a biscuit (whole or broken in half) in the bottom of an individual serving bowl and ladle a generous portion of gravy on top.

BLACK BEAN BURRITO BOWLS

Serves 4

If you are good at multi-tasking and comfortable with two burners and the microwave going at the same time, this dish comes together in about half an hour. Attractive and incredibly delicious on their own, these bowls don't even need tortilla chips if you want to keep them low-carb.

Ingredients

Quinoa:
- ½ cup rinsed quinoa
- zest of 1 lime (2 tsp.)
- juice of 1 lime, seeds removed (2 Tbsp.) + water to make 1 cup
- ¼ tsp. salt

Veggies:
- 1 Tbsp. olive or vegetable oil
- 1 green bell pepper, seeded and cut top to bottom in ⅛" thick strips (1 ½ cups)
- 1 medium white or yellow onion, cut top to bottom in ⅛" thick wedges (1 ½ cups)
- ¼ tsp. salt

Beans:
- 15 oz. can black beans, drained and rinsed
- 4 oz. can mild, diced, green chile peppers
- ½ cup frozen sweet corn
- 1 tsp. chili powder
- ½ tsp. ground cumin
- ½ tsp. ground coriander
- ½ tsp. garlic powder
- ¼ tsp. salt

Topping:
- 1 to 2 cups shredded cheese (4 to 8 oz.); pepper jack, queso, Mexican blend, cheddar, Monterey Jack, or mozzarella (use vegan cheese to make bowls vegan)

Serving:
- 1 cup sour cream for topping (optional)
- tortilla chips for scooping (optional)

Directions

1. **For Quinoa:** In a 1-quart saucepan, combine quinoa, zest, liquid, and salt. Cover.
2. Place pan over high heat and bring to a boil.
3. Stir and reduce heat to low. Cover pan and allow quinoa to cook, undisturbed, for 15 minutes.
4. **For Veggies:** While quinoa is cooking, place a large frying pan over medium heat.
5. Add oil and veggies to pan and sauté until onions are transparent and peppers are limp (10–15 minutes). Stir often.
6. After veggies are cooked, add salt and mix in.
7. **For Beans:** While quinoa and veggies are cooking, combine ingredients for beans in a 1-quart microwave-safe bowl. Stir.
8. Cover and micro-cook bean mixture on high until hot (3 minutes, stir, then 2 minutes more).
9. **To Assemble:** When all components are cooked, lay out four individual serving bowls (2-cup capacity). Divide quinoa between bowls – about ½ cup each.
10. Top quinoa with veggie mixture, dividing mixture equally between serving bowls.
11. Top veggies with bean mixture, dividing mixture equally between serving bowls – about ¾ cup each.
12. Top each bowl with a pile of cheese.
13. Serve bowls with sour cream and tortilla chips on the side, if desired.

Vegetarian Entrees

CHIK'N POT PIE

Makes 9" x 13" pan

If you want to make this both faster and lower-carb, skip the crust. Just pour the finished filling straight into the baking pan, top with the biscuits, and bake as directed.

Ingredients

Crust:
- 1 cup all-purpose flour
- ½ cup whole wheat pastry flour
- ½ tsp. salt
- ½ cup chilled butter, cut in cubes (1 stick)
- 4–6 Tbsp. cold water

Filling:
- 4 Tbsp. olive or vegetable oil, divided
- two 7.9 oz. packages vegetarian chik'n cutlets (8 cutlets total)
- 1 head fresh broccoli, diced (about 4 cups)
- 2 cups finely diced white or yellow onion (1 large onion)
- 2 cups finely diced celery (about 6 stalks)
- 2 cups shelled edamame (8 oz. package)
- 1 cup finely diced carrot (1 large or 2 smaller carrots, peeled)
- ½ tsp. salt
- 3 Tbsp. all-purpose flour
- 2 cups water
- 2 Tbsp. Better Than Bouillon vegetarian chicken flavor

Biscuit Topping:
- 1 ½ cups all-purpose flour
- ½ cup whole wheat pastry flour
- 2 Tbsp. granulated sugar
- 1 Tbsp. baking powder
- ½ tsp. salt
- 1 ¼ cups heavy cream

Directions

1. **For Crust:** In a medium mixing bowl, combine flours and salt.
2. Add butter to flour mixture. Cut butter into flour using a pastry blender or two butter knives, until mixture resembles coarse crumbs.
3. Add 4 tablespoons cold water to mixture and gently mix in with hands.
4. Grasp a handful of the mixture and squeeze gently. If it holds together, the mixture is ready; if it crumbles apart, add another tablespoon of water and mix in.
5. Gather dough into a rough ball, flatten slightly, place in a ziptop bag, and refrigerate for at least 30 minutes. Prepare filling while crust chills.
6. **For Filling:** In a large, 3-quart frying pan, heat 2 Tbsp. of oil over medium heat.
7. When pan and oil are hot, add the chik'n cutlets. Fry cutlets for about 5 minutes, flip, and fry for 5 minutes more. Remove cutlets from pan and set aside.
8. Return the frying pan to the burner and add the remaining 2 Tbsp. of oil.
9. When oil is hot, add the broccoli, onions, celery, edamame, carrots, and salt. Sauté the vegetables until the broccoli is tender-crisp (about 10 minutes). Stir often.
10. Add the flour to the vegetable mixture. Stir until no white spots of flour remain.
11. Add the water and bouillon to the vegetable mixture. Stir. Bring mixture to a boil, stirring almost constantly.
12. Remove vegetable mixture from heat. Cut the chik'n cutlets into cubes or thin slices and add them to the vegetable mixture. Gently blend in.
13. **To Assemble:** On a lightly floured work surface, roll the chilled crust out to a rectangle proportioned to fit the pan you are using (9" x 13" baking pan, or its equivalent). Use a rolling pin and roll the crust big enough to extend up the sides of the pan.
14. Transfer the crust to the baking pan. Gently press the crust into the bottom and corners of the pan. Tuck in any crust that sticks up above the pan and crimp the top edge of crust in a decorative manner.
15. Pour filling into crust. Spread to an even thickness.
16. Preheat oven to 400°.
17. **For Biscuits:** In a medium mixing bowl, combine all dry ingredients. Mix well.
18. Add heavy cream and gently mix in using hands. Mix only until a dough forms, or the biscuits will be tough from over-kneading. If dry flour remains at the bottom of the bowl, add a bit more cream to moisten.
19. Pinch off golfball-sized lumps of biscuit dough and shape each into a ball (you should have 15 balls). Make balls as even in size as possible.
20. Press each ball of dough into a disc ½" thick. Place discs on top of filling, spacing evenly.
21. Bake pot pie for 25 to 30 minutes, until biscuits are golden brown. Cut and serve.

EGGPLANT PARMIGIANA

Makes 8" x 8" pan; serves 4

I have been making eggplant parmigiana for a long time, but it is one of those dishes I used to make infrequently because traditional methods made it an all-day affair. I set out to remake this classic and develop a recipe that required minimal time and effort to prepare and was healthier than the traditional version that calls for battered, deep-fried eggplant. At last, this is it — simple ingredients, simple instructions, delicious results.

Ingredients

Eggplant:
- 2 medium eggplants
- 1 tsp. salt
- 3 Tbsp. olive oil

Sauce:
- 25 oz. jar marinara sauce (check ingredients and choose one with no sugar) or 2 ½ cups homemade marinara
- 1 tsp. dried basil

Cheese:
- 8 oz. provolone cheese, sliced or shredded (2 cups)

Directions

1. **For Eggplant:** Wash the eggplants and cut them crosswise into ½" thick slices, discarding the leafy tops and the very bottom pieces with the "belly button."
2. Lay the slices out on paper towels and sprinkle them with the salt.
3. Lay more paper towels over top, press lightly, and let sit for 30 minutes to draw out the bitterness. Remove and discard paper towels.
4. Preheat oven to 425°.
5. Brush olive oil on both sides of eggplant slices and lay them out in a single layer on a baking sheet.
6. Roast eggplant in oven for 30 minutes.
7. **For Sauce:** Open the jar of marinara sauce and add the dried basil to it. Stir to incorporate.
8. When eggplant is out of the oven, reduce oven temperature to 375°.
9. **To Assemble:** Layer ingredients in an 8" x 8" square baking pan, or its equivalent. Spread ½ cup of the marinara sauce in the bottom of the baking pan and top with half the eggplant slices.
10. Spread 1 cup of the marinara sauce over the eggplant and top with half the cheese.
11. Lay remaining eggplant slices over the cheese and top with the remaining marinara sauce.
12. Spread the remaining cheese over all.
13. Bake for 25–30 minutes until cheese is browned, and sauce is bubbly.
14. Remove from oven, slice, and serve.

"HAM" AND SCALLOPED POTATOES

Makes 9" x 13" pan; serves 6

Comfort food at its finest! The potatoes cook up tender and ridiculously good, with a nice hint of smokiness from the veggie ham. Cheddar cheese gives this dish a classic flavor — feel free to switch that up by using a different cheese or cheese blend. Better yet, use a smoked cheese to bring out that "meaty" flavor.

Ingredients

- 3 lbs. potatoes (8 fist-sized spuds), scrubbed and sliced ⅛" thick
- 1 large white or yellow onion, thinly sliced (about 2 cups)
- 5 oz. package veggie ham lunchmeat or two 6 oz. packages veggie bacon, diced
- 12 oz. shredded sharp cheddar cheese (3 cups)
- 1 tsp. salt
- ¼ tsp. black pepper
- 1 cup heavy cream
- 1 cup milk

Directions

1. Preheat oven to 350°.
2. In a 9" x 13" baking pan or equivalent casserole dish, place ⅓ of the potato slices in an even layer.
3. Top the potatoes with half the onions, half the veggie ham, and ⅓ of the cheese. Sprinkle everything on in even layers over the whole surface.
4. Top with another layer of potatoes (½ of the remaining pile).
5. Top these with the remaining onions, veggie ham, and half of the remaining cheese.
6. Lay the rest of the potatoes on top in an even layer.
7. Sprinkle the salt and pepper on top.
8. Pour the heavy cream and milk over all (it should rinse the salt and pepper down into the dish).
9. Cover the pan with aluminum foil or the lid to the casserole dish.
10. Bake casserole for 1 hour.
11. Take pan out of oven and remove cover. Top with remaining cheese, distributing it evenly.
12. Return pan to oven (uncovered) and bake 30 minutes more. Serve by scooping down through the layers.

INDIAN "MEAT"BALLS IN COCONUT CURRY SAUCE

Serves 6

I realize the list of ingredients for this dish looks a bit ridiculous. But if you read through the recipe and organize yourself, you can chop onions for both the meatballs and the sauce at the same time, open two cans of peppers, dump one here and one there, and put spices into the meatball mix at the same time you measure them out for the sauce. Really, it will save you a lot of time. Alternately, you can cook the meatballs ahead of time, refrigerate or freeze them, and then when dinnertime comes, all you have to do is make the sauce and the rice.

--- Ingredients ---

Meatballs:

- 14 oz. package vegetarian beef (as for making burgers)
- 8 oz. package tempeh, crumbled
- ½ cup bread or cracker crumbs
- 1 egg
- ½ cup finely minced white or yellow onion
- 4 oz. can mild, diced green chile peppers
- 1 Tbsp. minced fresh cilantro or parsley (or 2 tsp. dried)
- 2 tsp. garam masala (store-bought or from the recipe on page 151)
- 2 tsp. ground ginger
- 1 tsp. garlic powder
- 1 tsp. ground coriander
- ½ tsp. ground cumin
- ¼ tsp. ground black pepper
- ⅛ tsp. ground cayenne pepper
- 1 Tbsp. olive oil

Rice:

- ¾ cup brown rice
- ¾ cup quinoa, rinsed (or use all brown rice)
- 3 cups vegetable broth or water

Spice Blend for Sauce:

- 1 Tbsp. ground ginger
- 1 Tbsp. garam masala
- 2 tsp. ground coriander
- 1 ½ tsp. ground cumin
- 1 ½ tsp. ground cardamom
- 1 tsp. turmeric
- ½ tsp. dried mustard
- ½ tsp. ground celery seed
- ½ tsp. salt
- ¼ tsp. ground cinnamon
- ¼ tsp. ground cloves
- ¼ tsp. ground black pepper
- ⅛ to 1 tsp. ground cayenne pepper (your choice of heat levels)

Sauce:

- 1 Tbsp. coconut or vegetable oil
- 1 cup finely minced white or yellow onion (1 small onion)
- 1 Tbsp. finely minced or pressed garlic (3 large cloves)
- two 14 oz. cans coconut milk
- 4 oz. can mild, diced green chile peppers
- 6 oz. can tomato paste
- 1 Tbsp. lime juice (½ lime)

Serving:

- 2 cups cashews

Directions

1. **For Meatballs:** Preheat oven to 400°.
2. Grease a large baking sheet and set aside.
3. In a large mixing bowl, combine all ingredients for meatballs and mix gently with hands until thoroughly combined.
4. Form mixture into bite-sized balls (about 1 ½ Tbsp. each – a cookie scoop works great for this) and place on prepared baking sheet, leaving ½" space between balls.
5. Bake meatballs for 20 minutes.
6. **For Rice:** When meatballs go into the oven, start cooking the rice. Combine rice, quinoa, and broth in a 2-quart saucepan. Cover and place over high heat.
7. When rice comes to a boil, stir, reduce heat to low, and cover. Allow rice to cook, undisturbed, for 30 minutes.
8. **For Sauce:** While rice is cooking, make sauce. Measure all the ingredients for the spice blend into a ramekin or mug and set beside the cooktop.
9. Place a 3-quart saucepan over medium heat and add oil.
10. When oil is hot, add onion and garlic and sauté for 5 minutes.
11. Add spice blend, stir to incorporate, and cook until fragrant (less than one minute).
12. Add remaining sauce ingredients and stir with a whisk to fully incorporate.
13. Cover and bring sauce to a simmer (about 5 minutes), stirring often.
14. Add cooked meatballs to sauce and stir gently until all balls are covered in sauce. Reduce heat to low, cover, and simmer until meatballs are heated through.
15. Serve with a scoop of cooked rice in the bottom of individual bowls, a generous ladling of meatballs and sauce on top, and a sprinkling of cashews over all.

Vegetarian Entrees 103

LASAGNA

Makes 10" x 14" lasagna pan; serves 12

I won't lie, homemade lasagna is a labor of love. It takes time and effort to make, and with so many ready-made versions in grocery freezer cases, it is hard to justify making a pan from scratch. But, oh, the homemade stuff is so much better! This recipe is tried-and-true, and I promise, it is worth the effort to make. At day's end, it will bring your family and/or your guests incredible gustatory delight.

--- Ingredients ---

Sauce:

- 2 Tbsp. olive oil
- 1 medium or 2 baby eggplant, cut in ½" dice (about 4 cups)
- 2 medium yellow or white onions, cut in ½" dice (about 3 cups)
- 1 green bell pepper, seeded and cut in ½" dice (about 1 ½ cups)
- 8 oz. sliced mushrooms (about 3 cups, any variety)
- ¼ cup finely minced or pressed garlic (10 large cloves)
- 1 carrot, peeled and grated (about ½ cup)
- 12 oz. package ground veggie soy crumbles
- two 28 oz. cans diced or crushed tomatoes
- 12 oz. can tomato paste
- ¼ cup dry red wine (Cabernet Sauvignon or Merlot)
- ¼ cup vegetarian Worcestershire sauce
- 2 Tbsp. dried basil
- 2 tsp. salt
- 1 tsp. sugar
- 1 tsp. dried oregano
- 1 tsp. crushed red pepper flakes
- ½ tsp. dried thyme
- ½ tsp. ground black pepper

Cheese Layer:

- 16 oz. carton ricotta cheese
- 2 eggs
- 10 oz. package frozen, chopped spinach, thawed and drained
- 8 oz. shredded mozzarella (2 cups)
- ½ cup grated Parmesan cheese
- 1 Tbsp. dried parsley
- ¼ tsp. ground nutmeg

Pasta:

- 16 oz. box whole wheat lasagna noodles (15 noodles)

Topping:

- 8 oz. shredded mozzarella (2 cups)

Directions

1. **For Sauce:** In a 3-quart stock pot, heat oil over medium-high heat.
2. Add raw veggies – eggplant, onions, pepper, mushrooms, garlic, and carrots – and sauté until onions are translucent and peppers are wilted (about 10 minutes).
3. Add remaining ingredients for sauce, stir, cover, and reduce heat to low.
4. Simmer sauce for 1 hour, stirring occasionally.
5. Taste and adjust seasonings.
6. **For Cheese Layer:** In a medium mixing bowl, combine ricotta and eggs.
7. Mix with a fork or whisk until thoroughly blended.
8. Add remaining ingredients and stir to combine.
9. **For Pasta:** In a large stockpot, boil lasagna noodles just until al dente according to package instructions.
10. Drain and rinse quickly in cold water to arrest cooking process.
11. **To Assemble:** Spread 2 cups sauce in the bottom of a 10" x 14" non-reactive lasagna pan (no aluminum).
12. Top with 5 cooked noodles and then spread 4 cups sauce evenly over top.
13. Lay 5 more noodles on top and spread the cheese mixture in an even layer over this.
14. Lay 5 more noodles on top and spread the remaining sauce over top.
15. Sprinkle the cheese topping (8 oz. mozzarella) evenly over top of all.
16. **To Bake:** Preheat oven to 350°.
17. Bake lasagna for 45 minutes (uncovered) until cooked through, browned on top, and bubbly around the edges.
18. Remove lasagna from oven and let sit for 10 minutes before cutting into squares and serving.
19. If desired, lasagna may be made ahead and refrigerated or frozen before baking. Pre-made lasagna will keep up to 4 days in the refrigerator or up to 12 months in the freezer (allow to thaw before baking). If baking from a refrigerated or thawed state, bake for 60–70 minutes in a 350° oven.

MACARONI AND CHEESE

Makes 9" x 13" pan; serves 6 - 8

When my kids were little, I got my mother-in-law's recipe for a classic mac-'n-cheese. She wasn't quite clear on quantities, as she always made it by sight and touch, but I understood her instructions. And after I made it once — measuring everything as I went — I loved the beauty and mathematical simplicity of her method: 1 + 1 + 3 + 3 + 3. One pound pasta + one pound cheese + three tablespoons butter + three tablespoons flour + three cups milk. With very minor modifications, here is that recipe.

Ingredients

Pasta:

- 16 oz. dry macaroni (if using whole wheat pasta, add ½ cup heavy cream to cooked, drained pasta, before adding sauce)

Sauce:

- 3 Tbsp. butter
- 3 Tbsp. all-purpose flour
- ½ tsp. dried mustard
- 3 cups milk (for a lighter-on-the-dairy version, use: 1 cup milk + 2 cups water + 2 tsp. Better Than Bouillon, vegetarian chicken flavor)
- 16 oz. diced or shredded cheese (4 cups) – a mix of two or three kinds is best: 8 oz. Fontina + 4 oz. Asiago + 4 oz. muenster is fantastic; 8 oz. cheddar + 4 oz. American + 4 oz. mozzarella is the most kid-friendly
- ½ tsp. black pepper
- salt to taste

Topping:

- 1 cup grated Parmesan cheese
- ½ cup bread crumbs or cracker crumbs

Directions

1. Preheat oven to 350°.
2. **For Pasta:** In 4-quart stockpot, bring 2 quarts water to a boil and cook pasta according to package instructions, just until al dente.
3. When done, drain pasta and return to pot. While pasta is cooking, make sauce.
4. **For Sauce:** In a 2-quart saucepan, melt butter over medium heat.
5. Add flour and mustard to make a roux. Stir and cook for 2 minutes to eliminate raw flour flavor.
6. Add milk, whisk to eliminate lumps, and cook until sauce is bubbly and thickened.
7. Add cheese and pepper. Stir until cheese is melted and remove from heat.
8. Pour sauce over cooked drained pasta and stir gently until pasta is coated with sauce. Taste, and add salt, if needed.
9. Transfer mixture to a 9" x 13" baking pan and spread to an even thickness.
10. **For Topping:** Combine Parmesan cheese and bread crumbs and sprinkle over macaroni and cheese in baking pan.
11. Bake for 30 minutes until hot and bubbly.
12. Macaroni and cheese may be made ahead and refrigerated or frozen prior to baking. Cover tightly and allow to thaw before cooking.

MOSTACCIOLI

Makes 9" x 13" pan; serves 6-8

Mostaccioli is one of those dishes that is very forgiving and can be made from almost any meat or meat-like vegetarian protein + any sort of tomato or tomato sauce + any sort of melty cheese. Certainly, some combinations are better than others, but you get my point. Once my sons reached adulthood and were living on their own, they requested (demanded) several recipes, Mostaccioli chief among them. So then I had to, like, measure and stuff, and experiment with what was "best." With flavor and ease of preparation as my guiding principles, here is the resulting recipe.

Ingredients

Pasta:

- 16 oz. dry penne or rigatoni pasta (preferably whole wheat)

Sauce:

- two 12 oz. packages veggie chorizo (diced or crumbled), veggie bulk sausage, or ground veggie soy crumbles
- three 25 oz. jars spaghetti sauce or 8 cups homemade marinara sauce
- 1 Tbsp. dried basil
- ½ cup dry red wine (Cabernet Sauvignon or Merlot)

Cheese:

- 8 oz. shredded mozzarella or pepper jack cheese (2 cups)
- ½ cup grated Parmesan cheese

Directions

1. Preheat oven to 375°.
2. **For Pasta:** In a 4-quart stock pot, cook pasta just until al dente according to package directions. Remove from heat and drain. Return pasta to pot.
3. While pasta is cooking, prepare sauce.
4. **For Sauce:** In a large mixing bowl, combine all sauce ingredients. Stir vigorously, to break up veggie meat.
5. When pasta is cooked and drained, add sauce to pasta in pot. Stir gently to combine.
6. Transfer pasta mixture to a 9" x 13" baking dish and top with cheeses.
7. Bake for 30 minutes until mixture is bubbling and cheese is starting to brown around the edges.
8. Mostaccioli may be made ahead and refrigerated or frozen prior to baking. Cover tightly and allow to thaw before cooking.

SHEPHERD'S PIE

Makes 8" x 11" pan; serves 4-6

Hearty and filling, Shepherd's Pie is a classic for a reason!

Ingredients

Bottom:

- 1 Tbsp. olive or vegetable oil
- 12 oz. package ground veggie soy crumbles
- 2 Tbsp. vegetarian Worcestershire sauce
- 1 cup diced white or yellow onion (1 small onion)
- 1 cup diced carrots (2 large carrots)
- ½ cup finely diced celery (1 large rib)
- 2 tsp. finely minced or pressed garlic (2 large cloves)
- 1 tsp. dried thyme
- 2 Tbsp. all-purpose flour
- 1 cup vegetable broth (store-bought, homemade, or 1 cup water + 1 tsp. Better Than Bouillon vegetable or vegetarian chicken flavor)
- 1 cup frozen sweet corn

Top:

- 4 cups mashed potatoes (homemade, store-bought, or from a boxed mix)
- 1 cup grated cheddar or mozzarella cheese (4 oz.; optional)
- 1 egg

Directions

1. **For Bottom:** In a large frying pan, heat the oil over medium-high heat.
2. Add the veggie crumbles, Worcestershire, onion, carrots, celery, garlic, and thyme. Stir. Sauté until the onion is translucent (about 5 minutes).
3. Add flour. Stir in until no white spots remain.
4. Add broth. Stir, scraping any browned bits off the pan. Cook and stir until mixture is bubbling, and sauce is thickened.
5. Add corn, mix in, and remove pan from heat. Taste, and add salt if needed.
6. Transfer mixture to an 8" x 11" or 9" square baking pan and spread to an even thickness.
7. Preheat oven to 400°.
8. **For Top:** In a small mixing bowl, combine potatoes, cheese and egg. Stir with a fork or a whisk to combine.
9. Gently place dollops of potatoes on top of the veggie mixture and spread potatoes to an even thickness.
10. Bake pie for 25 minutes.

STROGANOFF

Serves 6-8

When I was newly married, my mother-in-law gave me a recipe for beef stroganoff, which used ground beef and canned soups. While tasty, her version had a lot of unhealthy ingredients in it from the convenience foods it contained. By contrast, my vegetarian version of this classic dish is healthy, flavorful, and easy to prepare. Best of all, the flavor and texture of the veggie crumbles is so good and beefy, this Stroganoff is hard to tell from its carnivore cousin. If you aren't a fan of noodles, serve this over cooked rice, baked potatoes, or toast.

Ingredients

Pasta:

- 12 oz. bag wide egg noodles

Sauce:

- 2 Tbsp. vegetable oil
- two 12 oz. packages ground veggie soy crumbles
- 2 Tbsp. vegetarian Worcestershire sauce
- 16 oz. package sliced mushrooms (about 6 cups any variety)
- 1 large white or yellow onion, finely minced (about 2 cups)
- 1 large clove garlic, minced or pressed (1 tsp.)
- ¼ cup all-purpose flour
- 1 tsp. paprika (sweet, not hot)
- ½ tsp. salt
- ¼ tsp. ground black pepper
- 2 cups milk
- 1 cup sour cream

Directions

1. **For Pasta:** In a large stock pot with a lid, set 3 quarts water to boil.
2. **For Sauce:** In a large frying pan over medium-high heat, heat oil.
3. Add veggie crumbles, Worcestershire, mushrooms, onion, and garlic to frying pan.
4. Cook, stirring often, until onion is translucent and mushrooms are almost cooked through.
5. Add flour, paprika, salt and pepper to mixture. Stir until no white spots of flour remain.
6. Add the milk, mix well, and reduce heat to low.
7. Cover, and allow sauce to simmer for 20 minutes while you cook and drain the noodles (follow package instructions).
8. Add sour cream to sauce and stir in.
9. Serve stroganoff on individual plates, in individual bowls, or from a common platter. Lay down a bed of noodles and top with stroganoff.

STUFFED PEPPERS

Serves 6

These peppers have so much going for them! Smoky and cheesy and basil-y, they are a far cry from those somewhat disappointing beef-and-rice stuffed peppers of your childhood. Thank heavens.

Ingredients

Peppers:

- 6 large bell peppers (green, red, orange, yellow, or a combination), washed, with tops cut off and seeds removed

Stuffing:

- 1 Tbsp. olive or vegetable oil
- 6 oz. package smoky tempeh or other veggie bacon, diced
- 1 cup finely diced yellow or white onion (1 small onion)
- ¾ cup brown rice
- ¼ cup wild rice
- 10 oz. package frozen chopped spinach, thawed (do not drain)
- 2 cups water
- 6 cloves garlic, finely minced or pressed (2 Tbsp.)
- ¾ cup pesto sauce (homemade or 7 oz. jar store-bought)
- 8 oz. smoked gouda or smoked mozzarella cheese, grated (2 cups)

Directions

1. Place peppers in an 8" square baking dish (or its equivalent), with open pepper tops facing up. If needed, shave a tiny bit off the rounded bottoms of the peppers to help them stand upright. Set aside.
2. Place a 3-quart saucepan over medium-high heat and add oil.
3. When oil is hot, add tempeh and onions. Sauté until onions are translucent (about 5 minutes). Stir often.
4. Add rices, spinach, and water to pot. Stir and cover.
5. When liquid comes to a boil, turn heat to low (2 on a scale of 1 to 10). Stir and cover.
6. Allow rice to cook, undisturbed, for 30 minutes. Check for doneness.
7. Preheat oven to 375°.
8. When rice is cooked and tender, remove pot from heat.
9. Add garlic, pesto sauce, and ⅔ of the cheese to the rice mixture. Stir in.
10. Fill prepared peppers with rice mixture.
11. Top peppers with the remaining grated cheese, distributing it evenly.
12. Bake peppers for 45 minutes. Serve hot.

SWISS MACARONI AND CHEESE

Makes one 9" x 13" pan; serves 6-8

I saw a travel show that featured the preparation of this dish. They gave no quantities or instructions, but after seeing it, I had to have it. I concocted my own version the next day, and, oh, it was tasty. Now, you can have some, too!

Ingredients

Onions:
- 1 Tbsp. olive oil
- 2 large white or yellow onions, thinly sliced (4–6 cups)
- 2 large cloves garlic, finely minced or pressed (2 tsp.)

Potatoes and Pasta:
- 1 Tbsp. salt
- 4 cups diced potatoes (peel only if skins are tough)
- 8 oz. whole wheat or whole grain dry elbow macaroni (2 cups)

Cheese Sauce:
- 3 Tbsp. butter
- 3 Tbsp. all-purpose flour
- 1 tsp. dried mustard
- 3 cups milk
- 16 oz. diced or grated cheese, best blend: 8 oz. gouda + 4 oz. Asiago + 4 oz. mozzarella (4 cups total)
- salt to taste

Topping:
- 4 oz. grated cheese (1 cup of one of the kinds used in the sauce)
- ½ cup bread or cracker crumbs

Directions

1. **For Onions:** In a large skillet over medium-low heat (4 on a scale of 1 to 10) cook onions and garlic in oil until caramelized. Stir occasionally. The onions must cook "low and slow" to develop the proper flavor, so start them first and allow them to cook the whole time you are preparing the rest of the dish.
2. **For Potatoes:** In a 4-quart stockpot, set 2 quarts water to boil over high heat. Prepare sauce while water heats.
3. **For Sauce:** In a 2-quart saucepan over medium-high heat, melt the butter. Add the flour and mustard. Mix to make a roux. Cook for 1 minute to cook out the raw flour flavor, stirring constantly.
4. Add the milk and stir with a whisk to incorporate.
5. Bring the sauce to a boil, reduce heat to low, and add the cheese(s).
6. Stir sauce until the cheese is melted and then remove from heat.
7. Preheat oven to 350°
8. **For Potatoes and Pasta:** When the pot of water is at a full rolling boil, add the salt and diced potatoes.
9. Cook potatoes until they are barely done (about 5 minutes).
10. Remove potatoes from water using a strainer or cooking spider. Place potatoes in a bowl and set aside.
11. Return water to a boil. Cook pasta until al dente according to package instructions.
12. Drain pasta and return to pot.
13. Add potatoes to pasta, along with onions and cheese sauce.
14. Stir gently to combine. Taste and add salt, if needed.
15. Transfer mixture to a 9" x 13" baking dish.
16. Combine the topping ingredients and sprinkle evenly over all.
17. Bake for 30 minutes.

TACO CASSEROLE

Makes 9" x 13" pan; serves 6-8

This casserole is a far superior dish if made with the homemade salsa beans. Making them requires time for simmering but very, very little effort or attention. Please give them a try!

Ingredients

Casserole:

- 12 oz. package veggie chorizo sausage
- 1 batch Salsa Beans from recipe below or two 15 oz. cans Kuner's Southwestern Black Beans with Cumin and Chili Spices + 1 can refried beans (any variety)
- 16 oz. jar salsa, your choice of variety and heat level (2 cups)
- 2.25 oz. can sliced black olives, drained (½ cup)
- 16 small corn tortillas (12 oz.)
- 16 oz. Mexican blend shredded cheese or your own blend of Monterey Jack and cheddar cheeses (4 cups)

Toppings:

- 8 oz. carton sour cream (1 cup)
- 1 – 2 cups shredded lettuce
- 2 cups halved cherry tomatoes (1 pint) or diced beefsteak tomatoes

Directions

1. Preheat oven to 350°.
2. In a large mixing bowl, crumble chorizo. Add beans, salsa, and olives. Stir until blended.
3. Grease a 9" x 13" baking pan.
4. Stack 8 corn tortillas and cut them into quarters.
5. Scatter tortilla pieces across the bottom of baking pan, distributing them evenly.
6. Top tortilla pieces with half the bean mixture. Spread to an even thickness.
7. Top beans with half the grated cheese.
8. Stack and cut remaining 8 tortillas and repeat layering process with remaining bean mixture and cheese.
9. Bake casserole (uncovered) for 40 minutes.
10. Remove from oven and cut casserole into squares. Serve topped with sour cream, lettuce, and tomatoes.

Taco Casserole is pictured on page 93

SALSA BEANS

Makes 7 cups

You can make this recipe using dried black beans if you have the time and want to save some money. Simply rinse the dry beans, soak them overnight, drain them the next day, and cook them (covered) with 2 cups water. After the beans are tender, add the salsa and simmer for 1–2 hours more. Cooked beans freeze well, so if you are taking the time to cook dry beans, consider making a double-batch to save time the next time you make the Taco Casserole. Or freeze the extra beans for another use.

Ingredients

- three 15 oz cans black beans, drained and rinsed
- 32 oz. jar salsa or 4 cups fresh salsa (your choice of variety and heat level)

Directions

1. Place beans and salsa in a 3-quart saucepan. Cover and place over low heat.
2. Cook, stirring occasionally, for 1–2 hours.
3. When done, the beans will have absorbed most of the moisture and all the flavor of the salsa. Taste and adjust seasonings.

Swellington Wellington, recipe on page 119

VEGAN ENTREES

This chapter is a love letter to my vegan brother-in-law. In my husband's family, there are all manner of eaters: carnivores, omnivores, pescatarians, vegetarians, and vegans. But where most are concerned, they are fast and loose with the rules — vegetarians who eat meat when not at home, self-professed carnivores who love vegan food, omnivores who won't eat beef or pork, etc. That is, with the exception of that one brother-in-law.

My vegan brother-in-law has not let any animal-related foods touch his lips in over twenty-five years. He loves food, loves to eat, and waxes poetic about his favorite vegan restaurants. He also arrives at family gatherings with his pockets full of nuts and power bars, accustomed to there not being much for him to eat, like he is too hard to feed. This upsets me, but I must admit that I, too, made rookie mistakes and was not always good at cooking for him. But I love him. And I learned. This chapter is for him and all the vegans out there who are absolutely delicious to cook for.

DOLMADES (STUFFED GRAPE LEAVES)

Serves 4-6

Stuffed grape leaves are traditionally stuffed with meat and rice, and this vegan version mimics the classic perfectly.

Ingredients

Wrappers:

- 16 oz. jar grape leaves
- 1 quart boiling water

Filling:

- 2 cups diced eggplant (1 small or baby eggplant, peeled and cut in ¼" pieces)
- 2 cups finely diced red onion (1 large onion)
- 1 Tbsp. finely minced or pressed fresh garlic (3 large cloves)
- 6 oz. jar pitted kalamata olives, drained and diced (about 1 cup)
- 12 oz. package vegan soy crumbles
- 1 cup dry orzo pasta (uncooked)
- 1 Tbsp. dried parsley
- 1 Tbsp. dried oregano
- 1 tsp. dried dill weed
- 1 tsp. salt
- ¼ tsp. ground black pepper

Cooking liquid:

- 2 cups vegetable broth or water
- ¼ cup lemon juice (1 large lemon)
- ¼ cup olive oil

Serving:

- 1 cup vegan plain Greek yogurt

Directions

1. **For Wrappers:** drain grape leaves, unroll, place in a baking dish, cover with boiling water, and let soak for 10 minutes. Keep leaves covered in water until ready to use, then drain.
2. **For Filling:** In a large mixing bowl, combine all ingredients for filling. Stir well.
3. **To Assemble:** Preheat oven to 375°.
4. Sort through leaves, removing any that are torn or very small. Use these to line a 9" x 13" non-reactive baking dish (no aluminum).
5. Lay out as many of the remaining grape leaves as will fit on your work surface. Lay them shiny side down, veined side up. Remove any stems.
6. Place 1 – 2 Tbsp. of the filling mixture in the center of each leaf (quantity of filling depends on size of leaf).
7. For each, fold stem end of leaf over filling, then fold in two sides of leaf and roll up, creating a small burrito shape.
8. Repeat with other leaves and place finished rolls in rows in the prepared baking pan. Pack rolls tightly against one another.
9. When filling and rolling is complete, drizzle rolls with the broth, lemon juice, and olive oil (in that order). If you have torn leaves leftover, lay them on top of the rolls.
10. Cover the pan with aluminum foil and bake for 60 minutes.
11. Serve Dolmades hot or warm, with plain Greek yogurt for dipping.

MASALA PEANUTS

Serves 6-10

My local Indian restaurant makes Masala Peanuts as an appetizer. They are incredible, way too hot for me, but also a bit addictive, and something I wanted to be able to make myself as an entree. After much trial and error, I have done it. My Masala Peanuts are saucier, seasoned a little differently than the restaurant, and just what I was going for. They are spicy-American-hot but not even close to authentic Indian-hot, so there you go.

Ingredients

Rice:
- 2 cups brown rice
- 4 cups water or vegetable broth

Nuts:
- 2 Tbsp. peanut or vegetable oil
- 3 cups finely diced white or yellow onions (2 medium onions)
- 4 cups roasted, salted peanuts (stray skins removed)
- ¼ cup mild Harissa (2 oz. Moroccan pepper paste)
- 1 cup water

Spice Blend:
- 1 Tbsp. garam masala (store-bought or from recipe on page 151)
- 1 Tbsp. ground ginger
- 1 Tbsp. ground coriander
- 1 Tbsp. ground cumin
- 2 tsp. garlic powder
- 1 tsp. ground turmeric

Finishing:
- two 28 oz. cans diced, fire roasted tomatoes
- 2 Tbsp. finely chopped fresh cilantro or basil
- ¼ cup lemon juice
- ¼ cup peanut butter
- ½ tsp. salt

Directions

1. **For Rice:** Cook the rice on the stovetop or in a rice cooker, according to the package instructions.
2. **For Nuts:** While rice is cooking, prepare the peanuts. In a large, deep frying pan (3-quart capacity), heat oil over medium heat.
3. Add onions and sauté until onions begin to brown (about 10 minutes).
4. Remove half the cooked onions to a bowl and set aside.
5. Into the pan with the remaining onions, add the peanuts, Harissa, water, and spice blend.
6. Cook and stir until peanuts are coated.
7. Cover pan, reduce heat to low, and allow peanuts to simmer for 30 minutes, stirring occasionally.
8. After simmering, add the tomatoes, cilantro, lemon juice, peanut butter, salt, and reserved onions.
9. Stir to combine and heat through.
10. Serve peanuts in individual bowls, ladled over portions of cooked rice.

SPAGHETTI WITH ROASTED VEGETABLE SAUCE

Serves 4-6

In the summer, when my garden is producing abundant vegetables, I make big batches of these roasted vegetables and freeze them in 2-cup containers — just the right amount for one batch of this sauce. Then, on days when time is short, this wonderful meal comes together in 30 minutes or less.

Ingredients

Roasted Vegetables:

- 1 large or 3 baby eggplant, cut in ½" dice (do not peel)
- 1 large green bell pepper, seeded and cut in ½" dice (about 1 ½ cups)
- 1 large white or yellow onion, cut in ½" dice (about 2 cups)
- 3 large cloves garlic, minced or pressed (1 Tbsp.)
- 1 jalapeño pepper (optional), finely minced (with seeds for heat)
- ⅓ cup olive oil
- 1 tsp. salt

Sauce:

- 1 Tbsp. olive or vegetable oil
- 12 oz. package ground vegan soy crumbles
- 2 Tbsp. vegan Worcestershire sauce
- two 28 oz. cans whole or diced tomatoes
- 6 oz. can tomato paste
- 1 Tbsp. dried basil
- ½ tsp. dried oregano
- salt to taste

Pasta:

- 13 oz. box whole wheat spaghetti or linguine

Cheese:

- 1 cup grated mozzarella-style vegan cheese

Directions

1. **For Vegetables:** Preheat oven to 425°.
2. In 9" x 13" roasting pan, combine all vegetables. Drizzle oil over top, sprinkle salt over all, and toss to combine and coat vegetables in oil.
3. Roast for 40–45 minutes, stirring once or twice in the middle of the cooking time.
4. **For Sauce:** In a 3-quart saucepan, heat the oil over medium-high heat.
5. Add the veggie crumbles, roasted vegetables, Worcestershire, tomatoes, tomato paste, basil, and oregano.
6. Cover, reduce heat to low, and simmer for 20 minutes. Taste and adjust seasonings.
7. **For Pasta:** While sauce is simmering, cook pasta according to package instructions.
8. Add drained pasta to sauce and gently stir the two together, or serve individual portions of plain pasta with sauce ladled over top.
9. Sprinkle grated cheese on top, as desired.

STIR-FRY WITH SPICY PEANUT SAUCE

Serves 6

I often make this dish when we are having guests for dinner, as it is delicious and universally liked. The sauce has a very mild kick of heat to it, which even young children like. And if you make the sauce 1–2 days ahead of time, this dish comes together quickly come dinnertime.

Ingredients

Stir-Fry:

- 4 Tbsp. peanut oil
- 14 oz. package extra firm tofu
- 8 oz. package mushrooms, sliced (3 cups any variety)
- 2 heads broccoli, cut into bite-sized pieces (about 4 cups)
- 1 large white or yellow onion, diced or thinly sliced (about 2 cups)
- 10 oz. spinach, fresh or frozen (if using frozen, no need to thaw or drain)
- 7 oz. package shelled edamame (about 1 ½ cups)

Peanut Sauce:

- ¾ cup natural peanut butter
- ½ cup coconut milk
- ½ cup soy sauce
- ¼ cup rice wine vinegar
- 3 Tbsp. brown sugar
- 3 Tbsp. lemon juice
- 1 Tbsp. sesame oil
- 4 large cloves garlic, finely minced or pressed (4 tsp.)
- 1 tsp. ground ginger
- ½ tsp. red pepper flakes

Pasta:

- 16 oz. package soba noodles (Japanese buckwheat noodles) or whole wheat spaghetti (use rice pasta for gluten-free)

Topping:

- 2 cups roasted cashews or peanuts

Directions

1. Remove tofu from package, drain, and slice horizontally into four slabs.
2. Place slabs on several layers of paper towels and allow to drain at least 30 minutes and up to 8 hours.
3. **For Sauce:** In a 1-quart saucepan, combine all ingredients for sauce.
4. Place over medium heat and cook, stirring almost constantly, until sauce is warmed, emulsified, and smooth. Do not boil or sauce will separate.
5. **For Pasta:** Fill a 4-quart stockpot half-full of water, add 1 tsp. salt, cover, and place over high heat. Do not add pasta yet.
6. **For Stir-fry:** Place a large, deep frying pan or wok over medium high heat and add oil.
7. When oil is hot, add slabs of tofu and fry until lightly browned (about 5 minutes). Flip, then fry until browned on the other side. Remove tofu, cut each slab into 8 pieces, and set aside.
8. In the oil remaining in the frying pan or wok, sauté all the vegetables, stirring frequently.
9. While vegetables are cooking, cook pasta according to package instructions. When pasta is al dente, drain it, and return it to the cooking pot.
10. When the vegetables are tender-crisp, add the cubed tofu and the sauce to the frying pan and stir.
11. Remove vegetable mixture from heat and pour over cooked pasta in pot.
12. Stir very gently until pasta and tofu-vegetable mixtures are integrated and pasta is coated in sauce.
13. Transfer mixture to a large serving bowl or platter and top with cashews or peanuts. Serve with tongs.

SWEET-AND-SOUR

Serves 6

I like my sweet-and-sour kind of soupy, so all those yummy flavors can soak into the rice. If you prefer your sweet-and-sour on the thick side, you will need to thicken this with cornstarch. At the end of the simmering time, add 2 tsp. cornstarch mixed with 2 tsp. water to the sauce. Stir it in, wait about 30 seconds, and voilà! Thick sauce! Thick or thin aside, if you choose to substitute fresh pineapple and fresh tomatoes for the canned, you will need to add ½ cup liquid to the pot — either apple juice or water.

Ingredients

Rice:

- 1 cup brown rice
- 1 cup white or red quinoa, rinsed
- 4 cups water

Sauce:

- two 8 oz. packages seitan strips
- 20 oz. can pineapple chunks or crushed pineapple in juice (not syrup)
- 14 oz. can diced tomatoes
- 1 medium white or yellow onion, thinly sliced (about 1 ½ cups)
- 1 green bell pepper, cut into strips ¼" wide and 1"-2" long (about 2 cups)
- 1 red bell pepper, cut into strips ¼" wide and 1"-2" long (about 2 cups)
- 2 Tbsp. grated fresh ginger (peel and grate on a microplane or the finest side of a box grater) or 2 tsp. ground ginger
- 1 Tbsp. paprika
- ½ tsp. salt
- ¼ tsp. red pepper flakes (optional)
- ½ cup soy sauce
- ⅓ cup honey or agave
- ¼ cup rice wine vinegar

Directions

1. **For Rice:** Cook rice and quinoa together on the stovetop or in a rice cooker, according to package instructions.
2. **For Sauce:** While rice is cooking, make the sauce.
3. In a covered 4-quart stockpot, combine all ingredients for the sauce.
4. Set pot over medium heat and bring to a boil. Reduce heat to low. Allow sauce to simmer for about 5 minutes, stirring gently a few times. When done, the pepper strips should be tender-crisp.
5. Serve rice in individual bowls with sauce ladled over top.

SWELLINGTON WELLINGTON

Serves 6

This vegan riff on a beef wellington is a beautiful medley of roasted vegetables and tender grains, wrapped in flaky puff pastry. Not difficult to make, it looks super-fancy when laid on a platter and paraded into the dining room. Just the thing for a holiday or special occasion.

Ingredients

Roasted Vegetables:

- 1 lb. parsnips, scrubbed or peeled and cut into ½" dice (3 cups)
- 2 leeks, white part cut in half lengthwise, then into ½" slices, soaked in water to release trapped dirt, then drained (3 cups)
- two 6 oz. packages smoky tempeh or other vegan bacon, diced
- ¼ cup olive oil
- 2 tsp. smoked paprika
- 1 tsp. dried thyme
- ½ tsp. ground black pepper
- ¼ tsp. salt

Grain:

- 1 cup pearled barley
- 2 cups water or vegetable broth
- ¼ cup red miso

Finishing:

- ½ cup golden raisins, minced
- 1 Tbsp. finely minced or pressed garlic (3 large cloves)

Pastry:

- 16 oz. package vegan puff pastry (made with vegetable shortening instead of butter)
- 1 Tbsp. vegan butter, melted

Directions

1. Preheat oven to 400°.
2. In a 9" x 13" baking pan, combine all ingredients for roasted vegetable mix. Stir to coat vegetables in oil and seasonings.
3. Roast vegetables for 60 minutes.
4. While vegetables are roasting, cook barley. In a 2-quart saucepan, combine barley, water, and miso. Cover pan and place over medium-high heat. Bring to a boil.
5. Stir barley, cover, reduce heat to low, and allow to simmer for 40 minutes, stirring occasionally.
6. Transfer cooked barley and roasted vegetables to a large mixing bowl. Add raisins and garlic to bowl. Toss and stir gently to combine ingredients.
7. On a lightly floured work surface, unfold puff pastry sheet. If package of puff pastry contains two sheets, overlap their long edges and press together to form one sheet of pastry. With a rolling pin, roll pastry out to a slightly larger size, keeping the thickness of the pastry even and the shape rectangular.
8. When the filling is cool enough to handle, place it in a pile down the center of the puff pastry (going the short way). With your hands, press the pile firmly together into a log.
9. Fold each side of the puff pastry over the filling. Pinch the seam together to seal. Pinch ends of pastry together to fully enclose filling.
10. Roll wellington over so the seam is hidden on the bottom. Transfer wellington to a parchment- or silicone-lined baking sheet.
11. Brush top of wellington with melted vegan butter. Make tiny slits in the top of the puff pastry for steam to escape. Do so in an artful pattern.
12. Bake wellington for 30 minutes (same temp) until the puff pastry is golden brown. Transfer to a serving platter, cut into 1 ½" thick slices with a serrated knife, and serve.

Swellington Wellington is pictured on page 113

VEGAN MACARONI AND CHEESE

Serves 6

It is a little unfair to call this dish "macaroni and cheese" because it doesn't contain cheese, but it truly is a vegan version of that classic dish, so there you go.

Ingredients

Pasta:

- 1 lb. whole wheat macaroni, rotini, penne, or other whole grain pasta

Sauce:

- 3 Tbsp. olive oil
- 8 oz. fresh mushrooms, sliced (any variety, about 3 cups)
- ¼ cup finely minced white or yellow onion
- 3 Tbsp. all-purpose flour
- 2 cups soy or oat milk, unsweetened and unflavored
- 1 cup vegetable broth (store-bought, homemade, or 1 cup water + 1 tsp. Better Than Bouillon, vegan chicken flavor)
- ½ tsp. black pepper
- 10 oz. vegan cheddar-style cheese
- salt to taste

Topping:

- 1 cup finely chopped walnuts

Directions

1. Preheat oven to 350°.
2. **For Pasta:** In 4-quart stockpot, cook pasta until al dente according to package directions.
3. Remove pasta from heat, drain, and return to pot.
4. **For Sauce:** While pasta is cooking, make sauce.
5. In a 2-quart saucepan over medium heat, heat olive oil. Sauté mushrooms and onions until onions are translucent and mushrooms are just cooked (about 5 minutes).
6. Add flour to mushroom mixture and stir until no white spots remain.
7. Cook for 1 minute to remove the raw flour flavor, stirring constantly.
8. Add milk, broth, and pepper.
9. Stir, scraping the bottom of the pan to prevent sticking and scorching.
10. Continue cooking sauce until mixture comes to a boil, stirring almost constantly.
11. Add cheese (broken into chunks) and cook sauce until cheese is melted, stirring constantly.
12. Remove sauce from heat and pour over cooked, drained pasta. Stir gently to combine. Taste, then add salt, if needed.
13. Transfer pasta mixture to a greased 9" x 13" baking pan and top with the chopped walnuts.
14. Bake for 30 minutes.
15. Macaroni and cheese may be made ahead and refrigerated or frozen prior to baking. Cover tightly. Will keep in the refrigerator for 4 days before baking, and up to 1 year in the freezer. Allow to thaw before baking.

"Bacon" Onion Rings, recipe on page 122

SIDE DISHES

I am an avid gardener, as I have been since I was about twelve and took over tending the family vegetable garden. I grew up on a farm, and there was plenty else for everyone to do, so I think my parents were grateful to turn the garden over to me. I like pulling weeds, so there was that, too.

When I was fifteen, growing zucchini was pretty new to the Midwest, and I decided to plant a dozen hills of the stuff. If you've ever grown zucchini, you know not to plant more than one hill and are busting a gut laughing right now. In my defense, I knew it was a squash, and my only experience was with winter squash, which produce a few fruits per vine. Zucchini is not like that. One plant produces enough to feed a neighborhood. Twelve hills? I had enough zucchini to fill the White House. We ate them at every meal, we froze them, we pickled them, and still there were enough to bury us alive. I called grocery stores to see if I could supply them, I set up a roadside farm stand, I tried to get the cows to eat them.

After weeks of "The Zucchini Situation," as everyone called it, things were so absurd, I felt like I had stepped into a Roald Dahl novel. I couldn't keep up with the harvest and started dumping the over-large zucchinis in a ditch behind the shop where my brother repaired machinery.

And guess what? After learning my lesson and planting just one hill the following summer, I discovered a giant patch of volunteer zucchinis behind the shop.

"BACON" ONION RINGS

Serves 4-6

I must confess to seeing this idea on the internet. Bacon + onion rings? Oh Lord of all that is good in this world, yes! Of course, none of the recipes I found suited me, and real bacon isn't going to fly on a pescatarian diet, so into the kitchen I went! It took some doing, but these are amazing and actually vegan! Touché!

Ingredients

Dipping Sauce:
- 2 Tbsp. ketchup
- 2 Tbsp. brown mustard
- 1 tsp. balsamic vinegar
- 1 tsp. liquid smoke

Onions:
- 3 large, sweet onions (red, Vidalia, or other)

Batter:
- 2 Tbsp. vegetable oil
- 6 oz. package smoky tempeh or other vegetarian bacon
- 1 cup all-purpose flour
- 2 Tbsp. cornstarch
- 1 tsp. baking powder
- ½ tsp. salt
- 1 cup club soda

Frying:
- 8 cups vegetable oil for deep-frying (64 oz.)

Directions

1. **For Dipping Sauce:** In a small bowl or mug, combine ingredients for sauce. Stir well. Set aside until needed.
2. **For Onions:** Cut the stems and roots off the onions. Peel the onions.
3. Cut the onions crosswise into ½" thick slices. Separate the slices into rings.
4. **For Frying:** In a stockpot, deep frying pan, electric fryer, or wok, heat oil to 375° (a deep-fry thermometer is invaluable). Oil should be at least 3" deep. Line a baking sheet with several layers of paper towels or newspaper, lay a cooling rack upside down on top of paper, and set aside.
5. Prepare batter while oil is heating.
6. **For Batter:** Place a large frying pan over medium-high heat.
7. When pan is hot, add 2 Tbsp. oil. Swirl pan to coat bottom in oil.
8. Add strips of smoky tempeh to pan. Fry until lightly browned on bottom (about 5 minutes). Flip and cook until lightly browned on other side (about 4 minutes).
9. Remove tempeh from pan and dice very finely (should yield 1 scant cup).
10. In a small mixing bowl, combine diced tempeh, flour, cornstarch, baking powder, and salt. Toss and stir to combine.
11. Add club soda to batter ingredients and stir gently until combined. Mixture will have small lumps in it.
12. When the oil is up to temperature, submerge several onion rings in the batter. Remove rings with your fingers or the tines of a fork and let the excess batter drain off.
13. Drop the battered rings in the hot oil. Be careful not to overcrowd the pan.
14. Cook each batch of onion rings for 3–4 minutes, flipping them over in the middle of the cooking time.
15. Remove cooked onion rings from oil with tongs or a kitchen spider and lay them out on the prepared tray to drain.
16. Allow oil to come back up to temperature before adding the next batch of battered rings.
17. Serve onion rings hot with dipping sauce.

"Bacon" Onion Rings are pictured on page 121

CORNBREAD STUFFING

Makes 8 cups

I know Pinterest inspires people to do crazy things with recipes, but sometimes, tried-and-true is truly the best. Like this recipe for good, old-fashioned, Thanksgiving-tastic stuffing. It contains nothing trendy or avant-garde and will never be labelled "fusion cuisine." Instead, it will make people happy and nostalgic. This stuffing benefits from the drying heat of an oven to crisp it up, so I would recommend against using it to stuff inside anything that would steam it instead.

Ingredients

- 8" pan cornbread (store-bought, from a mix, or homemade from the recipe on page 124)
- 2 cups frozen corn
- ½ cup finely minced white or yellow onion
- ½ cup finely minced celery
- 1 tsp. rubbed sage
- ¼ tsp. dried thyme
- 2 cups buttermilk
- 2 eggs

Directions

1. Cut cornbread into ½" cubes, place cubes in a large mixing bowl, and allow to dry out for at least 8 hours, and preferably for 24 hours. (If you are in a hurry, you can speed the drying process by using a warm oven. Spread the cubes out on a baking tray and place in a 200° oven. Check cubes after 2 hours.)
2. Preheat oven to 350°.
3. Add corn, onion, celery, sage, and thyme to cornbread cubes in bowl and toss mixture very gently with hands.
4. Add buttermilk and eggs and stir with a spoon until everything is moist and eggs are well-distributed.
5. Transfer mixture to a 3-quart casserole dish.
6. Bake for 60 minutes. Serve hot.

CORNBREAD

Fills 8" square pan

Cornbread recipes vary by the region of the country they hail from, so I need to declare that my cornbread is of the decidedly Midwestern persuasion. It is a little bit sweet (not too much; this isn't cake trying to pass for bread) and a whole lot of delicious. Just the thing to accompany chili or bean soup when there's a chill in the air.

Ingredients

- 1 cup yellow cornmeal
- ½ cup buckwheat flour or whole wheat pastry flour
- ½ cup all-purpose flour
- ¼ cup raw sugar, granulated sugar, or brown sugar
- 1 Tbsp. baking powder
- 1 tsp. baking soda
- ½ tsp. salt
- 2 eggs
- 1 cup buttermilk
- ¼ cup vegetable oil

Directions

1. Preheat oven to 400°.
2. Grease an 8"x 8" baking pan or 12 standard muffin cups and set aside.
3. In a medium mixing bowl, combine dry ingredients and mix together.
4. Add wet ingredients and stir just until blended and smooth.
5. Pour into prepared pan and spread to an even thickness.
6. Bake for 25 minutes until center springs back when touched.
7. Cut into squares and serve warm with butter, honey, and/or maple syrup, if desired.

VEGAN CORNBREAD

Fills 8" square pan

This corn bread has such wonderful flavor and texture, I have had vegans doubt my claims that this is safe for them to eat. I assure them it is, then contend that great vegan food should not be so surprising!

Ingredients

- 1 cup corn meal
- ½ cup whole wheat pastry flour
- ½ cup all-purpose flour
- ¼ cup raw sugar (if substituting honey, add it with the wet ingredients)
- 4 tsp. baking powder
- 1 tsp. salt
- 1 cup unsweetened oat, soy, almond, or cashew milk
- ½ cup apple sauce
- ¼ cup vegetable oil
- ½ tsp. vanilla

Directions

1. Preheat oven to 400°.
2. Grease an 8" square baking pan or 12 standard muffin cups and set aside.
3. In a medium mixing bowl, combine the dry ingredients and mix together.
4. Add the wet ingredients and stir just until smooth.
5. Pour batter into prepared pan and spread to an even thickness.
6. Bake cornbread for 25 minutes until center springs back when touched.
7. Cut cornbread into squares and serve with vegan margarine, honey, and/or maple syrup, if desired.

CREAMY COLESLAW

Makes 12 cups

I am a purist when it comes to certain things, and coleslaw is one of them. Where I praise creativity in the kitchen at other times, I frown upon it on Coleslaw Day. You will find no fennel, no poppy seeds, no hot peppers, no "new twists" in this dish. My coleslaw is old-school and BBQ-perfect, just like Grama's.

Ingredients

Dressing:

- ⅔ cup mayonnaise
- ⅔ cup buttermilk
- ⅓ cup apple cider vinegar
- 3 Tbsp. granulated sugar
- 1 ½ tsp. celery seed
- 1 tsp. salt
- ¼ tsp. ground black pepper

Veggies:

- 12 cups shredded green cabbage (2 lb. head)
- 2 cups grated carrots (2 large carrots)

Directions

1. In a very large mixing bowl, combine ingredients for dressing.
2. Stir with a whisk until smooth and homogenous.
3. Add cabbage and carrots and toss gently to coat veggies in dressing.
4. Cover, refrigerate, and let sit for at least 24 hours for cabbage to marinate and flavors to meld. Stir occasionally.

FANCY RICE

Makes 6 cups

I love rice made this way. The combination of sautéed onions, coconut milk, and cashews elevates humble rice to something extraordinary.

Ingredients

Rice:

- 2 Tbsp. olive or vegetable oil
- 2 cups thinly sliced white or yellow onion
- 2 cups brown rice
- 14 oz. can coconut milk (regular, not lite; 1 ½ cups)
- 2 ¼ cups vegetable broth (homemade, store-bought, or water + 2 tsp. Better Than Bouillon)

Finishing:

- ½ cup cashews, roughly chopped
- ¼ tsp. salt (more if broth and nuts are unsalted)

Directions

1. In a 3-quart saucepan over medium-high heat, sauté onion in oil for 5 minutes. Stir almost constantly.
2. Add rice, stir, and sauté for 1 minute.
3. Add coconut milk and broth, stir to incorporate, cover pan, and bring to a boil.
4. Turn heat to low and keep covered. Cook, undisturbed, until rice is done (30–40 minutes).
5. Remove from heat.
6. Add cashews and salt. Stir and serve.

FOCACCIA

Makes 11" x 16" flatbread

Foccacia bread is great either on its own or as a vehicle for flatbread sandwiches: cut the focaccia into squares, slice each square in half horizontally, and fill with your favorite sandwich makings. The focaccia toppings specified here are my favorites — feel free to swap them out for olives, roasted peppers, other herbs, or whatever! Exercise restraint, though — this isn't pizza!

Ingredients

Dough:

- 1 ½ cups water warmed to 105°-115° (should feel like warm bath water)
- 1 packet active dry yeast (2 ¼ tsp.)
- ⅓ cup olive oil
- 2 large cloves garlic, finely minced or pressed (2 tsp.)
- 1 tsp. garlic powder
- 1 ½ tsp. salt
- 2 ½ cups bread flour
- 1 cup whole wheat flour

Toppings:

- 2 Tbsp. olive oil
- 1 cup thinly sliced red onions
- 1 tsp. dried rosemary (1 Tbsp. fresh) or 1 cup grated sharp cheese

Directions

1. Place warm water in a large mixing bowl and sprinkle yeast over top.
2. Stir gently with a sturdy wooden spoon. Let sit, undisturbed, for 5 minutes until the yeast is dissolved and foamy.
3. Add oil, garlic, garlic powder, salt, and bread flour. Stir. After flour is fully incorporated, stir vigorously for 5 minutes more to develop the gluten and elasticity of the dough.
4. Add the wheat flour and mix in. Using hands, knead dough for 2 more minutes until the dough is slightly less sticky.
5. Pour 1 Tbsp. of the topping oil onto the center area of a 11" x 16" rimmed baking tray. Lay the dough on top of the puddle of oil. Pour the remaining 1 Tbsp. oil over top of the dough.
6. With your hands, gently press and stretch the dough to fill as much of the baking sheet as possible.
7. Allow dough to rest and rise for 1 hour.
8. With flat hands, gently stretch the dough to fill the whole baking tray. Be careful not to press down or deflate the dough.
9. Allow dough to rest and rise again for 30 minutes.
10. At this point, the dough should be double in height from the original. Press fingertips into the dough, creating a grid of indentations about 2" apart. Press your fingers in until you feel the baking sheet.
11. Scatter onions and rosemary across surface of dough, distributing them evenly.
12. Preheat oven to 400°. Allow focaccia with its toppings to rest and rise while the oven heats up.
13. Bake focaccia for 25-30 minutes until golden brown around the edges.
14. Remove focaccia from the oven and allow to cool at least 5 minutes before cutting into squares. Serve fresh from the oven or allow bread to cool completely.
15. Leftover focaccia freezes well in an airtight container.

FRIED GREEN TOMATOES

Serves 6

As an avid gardener, I swear there is nothing like going to the garden on a hot summer day, picking a ripe beefsteak tomato, and eating it on the spot. However, it takes so long for tomatoes to ripen, I find the waiting almost unbearable. Thus, I have been known to pick some of the earliest tomatoes while still green, fry them up for dinner, and end my agonizing wait.

Ingredients

Frying:

- 1 cup vegetable oil

Breading:

- ⅓ cup all-purpose flour
- 2 tsp. seasoned salt
- 2 tsp. onion powder
- 2 eggs
- 1 Tbsp. buttermilk
- ½ cup cornmeal
- 1 cup pulverized tortilla chips (blitz the bits from the bottom of the bag in a blender or food processor until they are fine crumbs) or fine bread crumbs
- ½ cup freshly grated Parmesan cheese

Tomatoes:

- 4 large, unripe (green) beefsteak tomatoes or 12 ripe tomatillos

Directions

1. Place oil in a 10" frying pan over medium heat.
2. On a medium plate or in a shallow dish, combine flour, salt, and onion powder.
3. In a small mixing bowl, whisk eggs and buttermilk together until homogenous.
4. On another medium plate or shallow dish, combine cornmeal, crumbs, and cheese.
5. Core tomatoes and cut them into ½" thick slices.
6. When the oil in the frying pan is hot, begin breading the tomato slices.
7. Dip a tomato slice into the seasoned flour, then the egg mixture, and then dip into the bread crumbs.
8. Lay the coated tomato slice in the hot oil and repeat the breading process with the remaining slices. Cook tomatoes in batches, as needed, so you don't over-crowd the pan.
9. Cook each batch of tomatoes for 4–6 minutes total, flipping slices in the middle of cooking time.
10. Remove cooked tomato slices to a paper-towel-lined plate to drain. Serve hot.

HUSH PUPPIES
Makes 34 two-bite fritters

I have tried a lot of less-than-great hush puppy recipes over the years and finally concocted my own to meet my "stringent" criteria — crispy on the outside, light and fluffy on the inside, and possessing good corny flavor. These are outstanding and a favorite of mine as a side dish for fish!

Ingredients

Frying:
- 8 cups vegetable oil for deep frying (64 oz.)

Batter:
- 1 ½ cups instant corn Masa flour (for tortillas) or cornmeal
- ½ cup all-purpose flour
- 2 Tbsp. granulated sugar
- 1 tsp. seasoned salt
- 1 ½ tsp. baking powder
- ½ tsp. baking soda
- 1 ½ cup frozen sweet corn
- ¼ finely minced white or yellow onion
- 1 cup buttermilk (or ½ cup sour cream + ⅔ cup milk)
- 2 eggs, lightly beaten

Directions

1. **For Frying:** In a stockpot, deep frying pan, electric fryer, or wok, heat oil to 375° (a deep-fry thermometer is invaluable). Oil should be at least 3" deep. Line a baking sheet with several layers of paper towels or newspaper, lay a cooling rack upside down on top of paper, and set aside.
2. **For Batter:** While oil is heating, mix up batter.
3. In medium mixing bowl, combine dry ingredients with corn and onion. Stir until well blended.
4. Add buttermilk and eggs and stir until combined. Do not overmix, or hush puppies with be tough.
5. When oil is up to temperature, drop golf-ball-sized balls of batter into oil (a cookie scoop works great for this). Do not crowd the pot. Cook the hush puppies in 2–4 batches, depending on the size of your pot.
6. Cook hush puppies for 4–5 minutes (until golden brown), flipping them in the middle of cooking time.
7. Remove hush puppies with tongs or a kitchen spider and lay on prepared tray to drain.
8. Allow oil to come back up to temperature before adding next batch of batter.
9. Serve hush puppies hot.

IRISH SODA BREAD

Makes 8" round loaf; 8 servings

Irish Soda Bread is incredibly quick and easy to make and lends itself to endless flavor variations. It is absolutely delicious fresh from the oven, but its one shortcoming is it dries out in just a few days and becomes not so delicious (unless you are hankering for a grilled cheese). Do not despair! I discovered this bread is fantastic as a stand-in for yeast bread in Thanksgiving Sage-Onion Stuffing. Cube any plain Irish Soda Bread that has lingered beyond the delicious phase and let it dry out completely — on the counter for a few days, or in a 170° oven for a couple hours — then proceed with the recipe on page 143. You will be amazed!

Ingredients

Batter:

- 2 ½ cups all-purpose flour, divided
- 1 ½ cups whole wheat pastry flour
- 1 tsp. salt
- 1 tsp. baking soda
- 2 cups buttermilk

Variations

Cheesy Irish Soda Bread

Add 2 cups shredded sharp cheese (8 oz. sharp cheddar, Asiago, gruyere, or other) + ¼ cup snipped chives (fresh or dried) to the dry ingredients.

Roasted Garlic Irish Soda Bread

Roast an entire head of garlic and add the roasted cloves + 1 cup grated Parmesan cheese to the dry ingredients.

Herbed Irish Soda Bread

Add ½ cup finely minced white or yellow onion + 2 Tbsp. dried rosemary + ¼ tsp. ground black pepper to the dry ingredients.

Sweet Irish Soda Bread

Add ¼ cup granulated sugar + 1 cup dried fruit (best: raisins, cranberries, currants, blueberries, or cherries) to the dry ingredients (break up fruit clumps). Top the finished loaf with 2 tsp. coarse or granulated sugar before baking.

Directions

1. Preheat oven to 350°.
2. In a large mixing bowl, combine 2 cups all-purpose flour and all the wheat pastry flour, salt, and baking soda. Mix well.
3. Add buttermilk and stir until dough comes together and forms a ball.
4. Place remaining ½ cup all-purpose flour on a work surface.
5. Transfer dough to the floured work surface and knead gently until the flour has been incorporated, but the dough is still covered in flour. The dough will be soft and wet.
6. Leave dough covered in flour and transfer to a greased baking sheet or 8" cast iron skillet.
7. Shape the dough into a round loaf about 6" in diameter and 2" thick.
8. With a sharp knife or a bench scraper, cut the loaf into quarters (cuts will make a +) leaving the four pieces in place, so the loaf is still round.
9. Bake bread for 45 minutes.
10. Cut bread into slices or wedges and serve while still warm with butter, if desired.

LEMON ORZO

Serves 6-8

Orzo cooks quickly, and this dish makes a perfect complement to virtually any seafood entree. Best of all, when you add the "fixin's" to the pot, your kitchen will fill with a heavenly aroma!

Ingredients

- 16 oz. dry orzo pasta (3 cups white or whole wheat)
- 2 quarts water for cooking + 1 Tbsp. salt
- 1 cup thinly sliced green onions (4–6 onions)
- 10 oz. package frozen spinach, thawed (do not drain)
- 2 tsp. fresh lemon zest (from 1 lemon) or 1 tsp. dried lemon zest
- ⅓ cup olive oil
- ⅓ cup fresh lemon juice (2 lemons), with seeds strained out
- 1 tsp. salt

Directions

1. Fill a 4-quart stockpot half-full of water. Add salt, cover, and place over high heat.
2. When the water comes to a boil, add orzo. Stir. Cook according to package directions until *al dente*.
3. While pasta is cooking, prepare the remaining ingredients.
4. When pasta is done, drain it and return it to pot.
5. Place pot over very low heat (2 on a scale of 1 to 10). Quickly add all remaining ingredients. Stir.
6. Cover pot and cook for 5 minutes for mixture to heat through. Stir several times. Serve hot.

MARINATED VEGETABLES

Makes 6 cups

I love this dish because it is such a delicious digression from steamed vegetables. I seem to make it a lot in the wintertime, as it employs canned staples I always have at hand. I love it also because it tastes best if made the night before serving, which saves precious minutes at dinnertime.

Ingredients

Marinade:

- 4 Tbsp. balsamic vinegar
- 2 Tbsp. wine vinegar
- 2 Tbsp. olive oil
- 1 tsp. dried thyme
- ½ tsp. salt

Vegetables:

- two 14 oz. cans artichoke hearts, drained and sliced in thin wedges
- 14 oz. can hearts of palm, drained (cut any large pieces in half and stalks into ½" slices)
- 6 oz. can pitted black olives, drained
- 4 oz. can whole mushrooms, drained
- 1 cup halved cherry tomatoes (½ pint), wedged beefsteak tomatoes, or ½ cup thinly sliced sun-dried tomatoes
- ½ cup thinly sliced red onion (¼ of an onion)
- ½ cup red bell pepper, thinly sliced or diced (½ of a pepper)

Directions

1. In a 2-quart covered container, combine all ingredients for marinade. Stir with a whisk or fork.
2. Add all vegetables to marinade. Toss very gently to combine.
3. Cover and refrigerate at least 6 hours before serving for marinade to penetrate vegetables.
4. Stir once or twice while vegetables are marinating.

MASHED POTATOES

Makes 8 cups

Mashed potatoes seem easy to make but aren't because so much can go wrong. Every potato is different, and under- or over-cooking the potatoes by even a little bit can ruin everything. Even recipes that specify the type of potato to use and include tips for success can go all kinds of wrong if the potatoes you are using have been stored under less than ideal conditions. I've included my best troubleshooting tips here to get you through the types of Mashed Potato Crises I have faced myself. But the best advice I can give you is to practice, practice, practice by making mashed potatoes a number of times to get the hang of it before making them to serve at a Grande Affair, like Thanksgiving.

Ingredients

Basic:

- 3 lb. bag red potatoes (unpeeled) or russet potatoes (peeled)
- water for boiling
- 1 Tbsp. salt
- ½ cup butter (1 stick) or ½ cup olive oil for vegan potatoes
- 1-2 cups warmed milk or 1 cup warmed unsweetened, unflavored oat, soy, almond, or cashew milk for vegan potatoes
- ½ tsp. salt

Roasted Garlic:

- 1-2 heads garlic
- 2-4 tsp. olive oil

Cheesy:

- 8 oz. shredded sharp cheese (cheddar, Asiago, or gouda)
- ½ cup shredded Parmesan cheese
- 2 Tbsp. snipped chives (fresh or dried)

Directions

1. Scrub potatoes if leaving skins on, or peel potatoes with a knife or vegetable peeler if skins are tough or if you want skin-free mashed potatoes.
2. Cut potatoes into large chunks – leave egg-sized potatoes whole and cut fist-sized potatoes in half. Chunks should be similar in size so they all cook in the same amount of time.
3. Place potato chunks into a 4-quart stock pot and fill pot with cold water just until water covers potatoes. Add 1 Tbsp. salt to pot.
4. Place pot over medium-high heat and cover.
5. Bring to a boil, then turn heat down to medium-low to prevent pot from boiling over. Keep water at a low boil and check potatoes for doneness after 20 minutes of cooking. Do this by stabbing one of the biggest chunks with a fork. Cook chunks until they are tender and a fork goes through them easily (30-40 minutes total).
6. Remove potatoes from heat and drain water off immediately.
7. Set the pot of potato chunks on a sturdy, heat-proof surface (can set them back on the warm burner, if desired). Add butter to the pot.
8. With a potato masher, mash the potatoes and butter together for about 1 minute. You should have a sort-of dry, lumpy mess at this point.
9. Add ½ cup milk and continue mashing until mixture is pretty smooth – should take about 3 minutes. NOTE: Don't over-mash the potatoes, or they will become gummy.
10. Add salt and another ½ cup milk. Stir in with a spoon.
11. Taste potatoes and assess. If they are lumpy, mash them some more or mix them briefly with a hand mixer but exercise restraint so they don't become gummy. If they need more salt, add it and stir it in. If they are dry, add more milk and stir it in with a spoon. If they are a total disaster, check the TROUBLESHOOTING tips on the next page.

Variations:

For Roasted-Garlic Mashed Potatoes: While potatoes are boiling, roast 1–2 heads garlic. Cut heads in half horizontally and coat each cut side with a small drizzle of olive oil. Put heads back together and wrap each head tightly in a small square of aluminum foil. Roast garlic in a 400° oven for 25 minutes. After mashing and seasoning potatoes, add the roasted garlic. Pop the roasted cloves out of their papery husks and into the potato pot. Leave garlic cloves in big pieces but stir potatoes vigorously to break up the garlic a bit and distribute it evenly. Let finished potatoes sit for 5 minutes before serving to allow the garlic flavor to permeate the potatoes.

For Cheesy Mashed Potatoes: After mashing and seasoning potatoes, add grated cheeses and chives. Stir. Cover and let sit for 1–2 minutes for cheese to melt. Stir potatoes again before serving.

TROUBLESHOOTING:

Overcooked, soupy, flavorless mashed potatoes: You lost track of time or cut the potatoes in tiny pieces to reduce the cooking time, and now you've got baby food. The very best fix for this is to add boxed Potato Flakes or Potato Buds to your runny mess. Add the flakes ¼ cup at a time, stir in, and give them 1–2 minutes to absorb the excess moisture. Add more, ¼ cup at a time, until the mashed potatoes are no longer soupy, and they actually taste like something. If your mashed potatoes are still a bit bland, or if the boxed potatoes gave the mix a "boxed" flavor, add onion powder 1 tsp. at a time. Also good for a flavor boost is bouillon – I love Better Than Bouillon, which is a paste, but 2 bouillon cubes softened in 2 Tbsp. hot water will do. If you don't have potato flakes on hand and don't have time to dispatch someone to the store, then cheese is your only hope. A mix of grated Parmesan and any sharp cheese is best, but beggars can't be choosers, so use what you've got. Add 1 cup grated cheese, stir in, and give it 1 minute to melt. Based on sight (Still soupy?) and taste (Have some flavor yet?), add more cheese as needed, adding ½ cup at a time. If the potatoes need a further flavor boost, add onion powder or bouillon (see notes above).

Gummy mashed potatoes: You beat the potatoes to death and over-mashed them in an effort to get them smooth, and now you have a sticky, gummy mess. Put the masher in the sink. Using a spoon, stir in ½ cup sour cream or plain yogurt (regular or Greek). Taste the potatoes. If that didn't fix it, stir in more sour cream or yogurt.

MEXICAN GRAIN SALAD

Makes 6 cups; serves 8

This recipe sounds unusual (cranberries? with beans?), but I swear you will not be able to stop eating this salad. Spicy and sweet and tasty, it is all good things. And even better if made at least a few hours before serving to allow the flavors to get acquainted. This salad can do as a main dish in a pinch, but I like it best when served alongside some quick quesadillas.

Ingredients

Salad:

- ½ cup rinsed white quinoa (or 2 cups leftover cooked quinoa)
- 1 cup water
- ¼ tsp. salt
- 15 oz. can black beans, drained and rinsed
- ¼ cup red onion, thinly sliced or ½ cup sliced green onions (2–3 onions)
- 1 cup dried cranberries
- ½ cup sunflower seeds
- 1 avocado, pitted, peeled, and diced

Citrus-Yogurt Dressing:

- ½ cup plain Greek yogurt
- 2 Tbsp. fresh cilantro, finely minced
- 1 tsp. finely minced or pressed garlic (1 large clove)
- 1 tsp. salt
- ¼ tsp. black pepper
- ¼ tsp. chili powder
- zest and juice of 1 lime (2 tsp. fresh zest + 2 Tbsp. lime juice)
- 2 Tbsp. olive oil
- 2 Tbsp. agave or honey
- ½ tsp. Frank's Red Hot Original hot sauce (or another mild, sweet hot sauce)

Directions

1. **For Quinoa:** In a 1-quart covered saucepan, combine quinoa, water, and salt. Place over medium-high heat and bring to a boil.
2. Stir, turn heat down to low, and cook quinoa for 10 minutes.
3. Turn heat off, leave pot covered and on the hot burner, and allow quinoa to steam another 5 minutes.
4. When done, remove quinoa from heat and transfer to a medium mixing bowl.
5. **For Dressing:** While quinoa is cooking, make Citrus-Yogurt Dressing. In a small bowl, combine all ingredients for dressing.
6. Stir with a fork or whisk until mixed and smooth. Set aside.
7. **To Assemble:** Add beans, onions, cranberries, and sunflower seeds to quinoa in bowl. Toss gently to combine.
8. Add citrus-yogurt dressing to bowl and stir gently until everything is evenly coated. Fold in diced avocado. Cover and chill until serving time.

MEXICAN RICE

Makes 5 cups

I find most restaurant Mexican Rice to be rather bland. This recipe will never be accused of that. Rich and complex, this dish retains the classic character of Mexican rice while featuring much more satisfying flavors. Serve this as a side dish along with refried beans to accompany any Mexican main dish.

Ingredients

Rice:

- 3 Tbsp. vegetable oil
- 1 cup brown rice
- 2 cups finely minced white or yellow onion (1 large onion)
- 1 Tbsp. finely minced or pressed garlic (3 large cloves)
- ½ tsp. chili powder
- 1 ½ cups vegetable broth (homemade, store-bought, or 1 ½ cups water + 2 tsp. Better Than Bouillon)
- 15 oz. can tomato sauce
- 4 oz. can mild, diced green chile peppers

Finishing:

- ½ cup frozen corn
- 2 Tbsp. fresh lime juice (1 lime)
- 1 tsp. salt

Directions

1. In a 2-quart saucepan over medium-high heat, heat the oil.
2. Add the rice, stir to coat kernels in oil, and sauté for 3 minutes, stirring almost constantly.
3. Add onion, garlic, and chili powder and sauté until onions are translucent, and garlic is fragrant (about 5 minutes).
4. Add broth, tomato sauce, and peppers. Cover and bring to a boil.
5. When rice comes to a boil, stir it, reduce heat to lowest possible setting, and cover.
6. Cook rice until it is tender (about 30 minutes), leaving it undisturbed.
7. When rice is fully cooked, stir in the corn, lime juice, and salt. Taste, adjust seasonings, and serve.

PASTA SALAD

Makes 12 cups

This salad easily transforms into a main-dish salad with the addition of protein: cubes of smoked mozzarella, pan-fried vegetarian chik'n cutlets cut into strips, pan-fried strips of seitan, or cooked shrimp.

Ingredients

Salad:

- 13 oz. package whole wheat rotini, elbow macaroni, penne, or rigatoni
- 10 oz. package frozen chopped spinach, thawed and drained
- ½ tsp. salt
- 2 cups halved cherry tomatoes (1 pint) or diced beefsteak tomato
- 6"–8" cucumber, scrubbed and diced (about 2 cups)
- 1 cup thinly sliced red onion or sliced green onions

Dressing:

- 1 ½ cups Italian vinaigrette (store-bought or homemade from recipe on page 155)

Directions

1. Cook the pasta just until al dente, according to the package instructions.
2. Drain pasta immediately and rinse briefly in cold water.
3. Transfer the drained pasta to a large mixing bowl. Add the spinach, salt, and vinaigrette. With a rubber spatula, stir to coat the pasta and to bust up any lumps of spinach.
4. Add remaining ingredients to bowl. Gently fold together.
5. Cover salad and chill until serving time. Stir again before serving.

POTATO SALAD

Makes 10 cups

Using thin-skinned potatoes in this Potato Salad means tender skins and no need to peel, which is a huge time-savings. Be sure to keep this chilled, as mayonnaise and cooked eggs are not to be trifled with on a hot summer day at a picnic.

Ingredients

- 3 lbs. thin-skinned red, golden, or other non-russet potatoes (8 fist-sized spuds)
- 4 eggs
- 1 cup mayonnaise
- ¾ cup sweet pickle relish
- 1 Tbsp. brown or Dijon-style mustard
- 2 tsp. ground celery seeds
- 1 tsp. salt

Directions

1. Scrub potatoes but do not peel.
2. Prick each potato in two places with a fork or sharp knife to prevent explosions.
3. Bake potatoes either in a 350° oven for 45–60 minutes (depending on potato size) or in the microwave.
4. **To Microwave:** Lay potatoes in concentric rings on the glass cooking platform. Micro-cook on high for 8 minutes. Turn potatoes over (flip so the side of the potato that was facing outward is now facing inward) and cook on high for 8 minutes more. If potatoes aren't fully cooked, micro-cook in 2-minute bursts until they are. When done, potatoes will not resist the stab of a fork.
5. Allow cooked potatoes to cool.
6. **For Eggs:** While potatoes are cooking, hard-boil the eggs – instructions on page 3, if needed. Peel when cool.
7. **To Assemble:** Cut cooled potatoes into ¾" cubes and transfer to a large mixing bowl.
8. Chop hard-boiled eggs and add to potatoes in bowl.
9. Add remaining ingredients and stir gently with a rubber spatula until thoroughly blended.
10. Taste, adjust seasonings, cover, and refrigerate. Serve chilled.

Side Dishes

QUINOA WITH RAISINS AND PEPITAS

Makes 3 cups

I love quinoa because it tastes great, cooks quickly, absorbs whatever flavors you throw at it, and is a grain with a high-protein content (it contains all the essential amino acids). Here, it is the main attraction in a simple but stupendous side dish.

Ingredients

- 1 cup rinsed quinoa (white or red)
- 2 cups vegetable broth (homemade, store-bought, or 2 cups water + 2 tsp. Better Than Bouillon vegetarian chicken or vegetable flavor)
- ¼ cup raisins (regular or golden)
- 2 Tbsp. pepitas (pumpkin seeds)

Directions

1. In a 2-quart saucepan, combine quinoa, broth, and raisins.
2. Cover and place over medium-high heat. Bring to a boil.
3. Stir, reduce heat to lowest possible setting, and cover.
4. Allow quinoa to simmer for 15 minutes until all liquid is absorbed.
5. Remove pan from heat. Stir in pepitas.
6. Taste and add salt if needed. Serve hot.

SWEET POTATO FRIES

Makes 4 cups

These are so good and so easy, I make them (literally) all the time. They go with everything, plus sweet potatoes are a healthy superfood.

Ingredients

- 3 lb. bag sweet potatoes, peeled and rinsed (about 8 fist-sized spuds)
- ¼ cup olive oil
- 1 Tbsp. smoked sea salt (available from a variety of retailers)

Directions

1. Preheat oven to 425°.
2. Cut the peeled potatoes lengthwise into ¼" thick slices.
3. Cut the slices lengthwise into ¼" sticks.
4. Transfer the potato sticks to a large baking sheet and drizzle olive oil over top.
5. Sprinkle salt over potato sticks. Gently toss and stir sticks to coat them in oil and salt. Spread fries out to an even layer on baking sheet.
6. Bake fries for 30 minutes total. Stir once, after 10 minutes of baking, and then leave fries undisturbed.
7. Remove fries from oven and serve hot.

REFRIED BEANS

Makes 6 cups

Refried Beans are so versatile, I make big batches of them and freeze them in small containers to have on hand for a variety of meals. So much better than the canned kind, I make nachos, burritos, quesadillas, and more with them. Refried Beans + Mexican Rice also make a classic accompaniment for a variety of Mexican meals.

Ingredients

- 1 lb. dried pinto beans
- water for soaking
- 2 cups vegetable broth or water
- 1 large white or yellow onion, diced (2 cups)
- 2 large cloves garlic, finely minced or pressed (2 tsp.)
- 1 tsp. ground cumin
- ½ tsp. ground coriander
- 1 Tbsp. butter or vegetable oil
- 2 oz. sharp cheddar cheese, diced (½ cup)
- 2 Tbsp. ketchup
- salt to taste

Directions

1. Place dried beans in a colander. Sort through them and remove any stones or debris. Rinse beans thoroughly while agitating them to release dirt.
2. Transfer beans to a 4-quart stock pot and add cold water to a depth twice that of the beans. Cover and allow to soak overnight.
3. The next day, drain beans and return them to the pot. (If you forget to soak the beans overnight, you can accelerate the soaking process by rinsing the beans and placing them in a stockpot with cold water covering the beans by 2". Cover pot, bring to a boil, boil for two minutes, turn off the heat, and let stand for 2 hours. Drain, rinse, and return to pot. Add 60 minutes to overall cooking time if using the quick-soak method.)
4. Add broth to beans in pot.
5. Cover, place over high heat, and bring to a boil.
6. Reduce heat to low, add onion, garlic, cumin, and coriander.
7. Cover and allow beans to simmer until fully cooked and soft (about 1 hour), stirring occasionally.
8. When beans are tender, mash lightly with a potato masher, and add remaining ingredients. Stir until cheese and butter are melted and incorporated.
9. Taste and adjust seasonings. Extra beans freeze well if stored in airtight containers.

SCONES

Makes 12

Every few years, I seem to have a scone fit, making one variety or another for practically every occasion. Eventually, everyone gets tired of "scones again," and I move on, sadly forgetting how absolutely terrific and versatile scones are. But then, the fit comes on once again.

Ingredients

- 3 cups all-purpose flour
- ⅓ cup granulated sugar
- 1 Tbsp. baking powder
- ½ tsp. baking soda
- ½ tsp. salt
- ½ cup cold butter (1 stick)
- 1 cup buttermilk
- 2 eggs

Directions

1. Preheat oven to 400°.
2. In a large mixing bowl, combine flour, sugar, baking powder, soda, and salt. Mix well.
3. Cut butter in, using a food processor, pastry cutter, or two forks. Mixture should resemble coarse crumbs.
4. Add buttermilk and eggs and mix with hands just until combined. Don't over-mix or the scones will be tough.
5. Divide dough in half and transfer to a well-floured work surface.
6. Sprinkle tops of dough mounds with flour. Shape each mound into a disc 6" in diameter and 1" thick.
7. Cut each disc into 6 wedges. Transfer wedges to a baking sheet, placing the wedges at least 1" apart.
8. Bake for 20–25 minutes until the scones are firm to the touch and just beginning to brown.
9. Serve scones plain or with butter and clotted cream.

Variations

Savory Scones: Reduce sugar to ¼ cup and add 2–4 Tbsp. fresh snipped herbs to the batter after cutting in butter. Dip tops of scones in grated Parmesan cheese before baking.

Cheese scones: Reduce sugar to ¼ cup and add 1 cup grated sharp cheddar cheese (4 oz.), 1 tsp. onion powder, and 1 Tbsp. dried parsley to the batter after cutting in butter. Top with ½ cup grated sharp cheddar cheese (2 oz.) before baking.

Sweet Scones: Add 1 cup dried fruit (1 cup raisins + 1 Tbsp. cinnamon or 1 cup dried cranberries + 1 Tbsp. orange zest are both excellent!) to batter after cutting in butter and sprinkle tops of scones with raw or granulated sugar before baking (with or without an egg wash first).

Blueberry Scones: Add 1 cup dried blueberries and 1 tsp. fresh lemon zest (or ½ tsp. dried) to batter. Glaze the finished scones while warm.

Lemon glaze:

- 2 Tbsp. melted butter
- 2 Tbsp. confectioner's sugar
- 2 Tbsp. lemon juice

In small bowl, combine ingredients and mix until smooth.

THANKSGIVING SAGE-ONION STUFFING

Makes 12 cups

We never seem to eat that last crust of bread, and I hate waste, so I cube up those last pieces, let them sit in a bowl on the counter to dry out, and toss all the dried bread cubes in a bag. When the bag is full, I make a batch of this stuffing. This is also my go-to recipe for Thanksgiving. I like my stuffing baked in a casserole, with crispy bits on the edges, but this stuffing is also delicious stuffed inside other things and baked to a softer, steamier consistency.

Ingredients

- 12 cups dried bread cubes (assorted kinds of bread is fine)
- 1 ½ cups very finely minced onion
- 3 Tbsp. dried sage
- 3 eggs, lightly beaten
- 1 stick butter, melted (8 Tbsp.)
- 2 cups vegetable broth (homemade, store-bought, or 2 cups water + 2 tsp. Better Than Bouillon vegetable or vegetarian chicken flavor)
- 2–3 cups milk

Directions

1. In a very large mixing bowl, place bread cubes, onion, and sage.
2. Toss gently once or twice to begin to combine ingredients.
3. Add eggs, butter, vegetable stock, and 2 cups milk and stir gently until thoroughly combined. If using unsalted butter and low-sodium broth, add ½ tsp. salt to mixture.
4. Depending on the bread used, more milk may be required. The stuffing mixture should be coated and slightly moist, with some liquid left standing in the bottom of the bowl. If this is not the case, add more milk (½ cup at a time) until it is. Do not wait to make this assessment, as the bread will absorb the standing liquid rather quickly.
5. Allow mixture to sit at room temperature for 2 hours before baking. This allows the moisture to absorb and disperse evenly throughout the mixture.
6. Preheat oven to 350°.
7. Transfer stuffing mixture to a casserole dish.
8. Bake, uncovered, for 60 minutes.
9. When done, stuffing will be browned on top and no longer squishy in the middle (touch top of stuffing to test).

VEGAN BAKED BEANS
Makes 12 cups

The perfect side dish for a cook-out to accompany veggie burgers and tofu dogs, this baked-bean recipe makes a big, delicious batch. Beans freeze well, so I often make a batch of these "just for us" and freeze the leftovers in meal-sized portions.

Ingredients

- 2 lbs. dried navy beans
- water for soaking
- 5 cups vegetable broth or water (may use 1 bottle dark beer for part of the liquid)
- 2 large white or yellow onions, diced (4–6 cups)
- ½ cup brown sugar
- 1 ½ cups ketchup
- ½ cup molasses
- 2 Tbsp. apple cider vinegar
- 1 ½ tsp. liquid smoke
- 3 Tbsp. mustard powder
- 1 bay leaf
- 1 tsp. salt
- ½ tsp. ground black pepper
- ¼ tsp. cayenne pepper

Directions

1. Place dried beans in a colander. Sort through them and remove any stones or debris. Rinse beans thoroughly while agitating them to release dirt.
2. Transfer beans to a 6-quart stockpot and add cold water to a depth twice that of the beans. Cover and allow to soak overnight.
3. The next day, drain beans and return them to the pot. (If you forget to soak the beans overnight, you can accelerate the soaking process by rinsing beans and placing in stockpot with cold water covering the beans by 2". Cover pot, bring to a boil, boil for two minutes, turn off the heat, and let stand for 2 hours. Drain, rinse, and return to pot. Add 1 hour to overall cooking time if using the quick-soak method.)
4. Add broth to beans in pot.
5. Cover and place pot over medium-high heat. Bring to a boil.
6. Reduce heat to low. Allow mixture to simmer for 1 hour. Stir occasionally.
7. Beans should be tender but not completely cooked and mushy. Add the remaining ingredients. Stir in.
8. Reduce heat to lowest possible setting. Allow beans to simmer (covered) an additional 1–2 hours (until flavors have penetrated beans) stirring occasionally. Alternately, you can "simmer" the beans in the oven. Transfer the beans and seasonings to a covered casserole dish or dutch oven. Bake for 2–4 hours in a 325° oven. No need to stir.
9. Taste and adjust seasonings.
10. Serve baked beans hot or at room temperature. Refrigerate or freeze any leftovers.

DRY RUBS AND SEASONINGS

Dry rubs and seasoning blends are two of the greatest time-savers in the kitchen. If made ahead and kept on hand, a seasoning blend allows you to dress up a dish in seconds. And dry rubs are my favorite trick for getting a superb dinner on the table in 15 minutes flat. Here's how:

TO COOK FISH: Bake — preheat oven to 350°. Pat raw fish filets dry with a paper towel. Place fish on a greased baking sheet and drizzle or spritz with a small amount of vegetable oil. Sprinkle desired dry rub over surface of fish, at the rate indicated on the recipe. Bake fish for 10 minutes per inch of thickness. **Pan fry** — dry and season fish as above. Heat a heavy frying pan over medium-high heat and add vegetable or olive oil to pan (2 Tbsp. oil per pound of fish). When oil is hot, add fish fillets in a single layer (cook in batches, if necessary) and allow to cook, undisturbed, for 2 – 3 minutes (shake pan — when fish is ready to flip, it will slide free). Flip fish over and cook 2 – 3 minutes more. **Grill** — dry and season fish as above. Place fish fillets on a greased, perforated pan (a disposable foil baking pan that you have stabbed with a fork or knife works great), over medium coals. Cover grill and allow fish to cook for 10 minutes per inch of thickness.

TO COOK SHRIMP: Bake — preheat oven to 350°. Peel and de-vein shrimp. Pat dry and place in a bowl. Drizzle with vegetable oil (1 Tbsp. oil per pound of shrimp) and apply rub at rate indicated on the recipe. Stir to coat shrimp. Spread the seasoned shrimp out in a single layer on a greased baking sheet. Bake for 15 minutes, until shrimp are pink and firm. **Pan fry** — heat a heavy frying pan over medium-high heat and add vegetable or olive oil to pan (1 Tbsp. oil per pound of shrimp). When oil is hot, add shrimp in a single layer (cook in batches, if necessary) and allow them to cook, undisturbed, for 2 – 3 minutes. Flip and cook 2 – 3 minutes more. Shrimp will be pink and firm when done. **Grill** — thread seasoned shrimp on skewers or place shrimp in a greased grill pan. Place over medium coals and cook for about 5 minutes total, flipping halfway through.

CAJUN RUB
Makes 5 tablespoons
(enough to season 5 pounds of meat)

Full-flavored with just a bit of heat. Excellent on most any seafood, but especially on shrimp (peeled and de-veined) or any white-fleshed fish.

Ingredients
- 1 bay leaf, broken into small pieces
- ½ tsp. salt
- 1 Tbsp. smoked paprika
- 1 Tbsp. celery salt
- 1 Tbsp. dried parsley
- 2 tsp. onion powder
- 2 tsp. garlic powder
- 1 tsp. black pepper
- ½ tsp. cayenne pepper
- ½ tsp. dried oregano
- ¼ tsp. dried sage

Directions
1. With a mortar and pestle, or in a coffee grinder, pulverize the bay leaf and salt together. Transfer mixture to a small bowl.
2. Add remaining ingredients to bowl and stir with a whisk to mix thoroughly.
3. Transfer mixture to a spice jar or other airtight container and label. Rub will maintain its flavor for a year at room temperature and longer if stored in the freezer.
4. **To Use:** Apply rub to raw fish or shellfish at a rate of 1 Tbsp. seasoning per pound of meat. See page 145 for cooking instructions.

CHINESE 12-SPICE RUB
Makes ½ cup
(enough to season 4 pounds of meat)

This distinctive rub is best on a dark-fleshed fish like tuna or salmon. The ginger and cayenne give it a bit of a kick, and the other spices create a robust, complex base of flavors.

Ingredients
- 3 Tbsp. Chinese 5-spice powder (cinnamon, anise, allspice, fennel, cloves)
- 2 Tbsp. ground ginger
- 1 Tbsp. onion powder
- 1 Tbsp. granulated sugar
- 2 tsp. garlic powder
- 1 tsp. ground turmeric
- 1 tsp. salt
- ½ tsp. ground coriander
- ¼ tsp. ground black pepper
- ⅛ tsp. ground cayenne pepper

Directions
1. In a small bowl, combine all ingredients and mix with a whisk.
2. Transfer mixture to a spice jar or other airtight container and label. Rub will maintain its flavor for a year at room temperature and longer if stored in the freezer.
3. **To Use:** Apply rub to raw fish at a rate of 2 Tbsp. seasoning per pound of meat. See page 145 for cooking instructions.

HOT MUSTARD RUB
Makes 5 tablespoons (enough to season 2 ½ pounds of meat)

Sweet and hot — fantastic on salmon or really, any fish.

Ingredients
- 2 Tbsp. Colman's ground dry mustard
- 2 Tbsp. raw sugar
- 1 tsp. dried dill weed
- 1 tsp. salt
- ½ tsp. turmeric
- ¼ tsp. cayenne pepper

Directions
1. In a small bowl, combine all ingredients and mix with a whisk.
2. Transfer mixture to a spice jar or other airtight container and label.
3. Rub will maintain its flavor for a year at room temperature and longer if stored in the freezer.
4. **To Use:** Apply rub to raw fish at a rate of 2 Tbsp. seasoning per pound of meat. See page 145 for cooking instructions.

INDIAN RUB

Makes ½ cup
(enough to season 8 pounds of meat)

Indian recipes tend to be incredibly delicious but time-consuming, with ingredient lists as long as my leg, and instructions even longer. This recipe is my answer in the affirmative to the question, "Is there an easier way?" Full of authentic flavor, with none of the authentic effort, this rub is fantastic on shrimp or any kind of fish.

Ingredients

- 3 Tbsp. onion powder
- 2 Tbsp. dried cilantro
- 1 Tbsp. dried ground ginger
- 1 Tbsp. salt
- 2 tsp. garlic powder
- 2 tsp. garam masala (store-bought or from recipe on page 151)
- 1 tsp. turmeric
- 1 tsp. cumin
- ½ tsp. cayenne pepper
- ½ tsp. black pepper

Directions

1. In a small bowl, combine all ingredients and mix with a whisk.
2. Transfer mixture to a spice jar or other airtight container and label. Rub will maintain its flavor for a year at room temperature and longer if stored in the freezer.
3. **To Use:** Apply rub to raw fish or shellfish at a rate of 2 Tbsp. seasoning per pound of meat. See page 145 for cooking instructions.

TEXAS RUB

Makes 8 tablespoons
(enough to season 4 pounds of seafood or vegetarian burgers)

This rub imparts a complex, smoky spice profile to any veggie burger or seafood. Especially good on any dish that is to be grilled or smoked.

Ingredients

- 1 dried bay leaf, broken into small pieces
- 1 Tbsp. smoked sea salt
- 1 Tbsp. onion powder
- 1 Tbsp. garlic powder
- 1 Tbsp. chili powder
- 1 Tbsp. smoked paprika
- 1 Tbsp. ground cumin
- 1 Tbsp. ground black pepper
- 1 ½ tsp. Colman's dried mustard powder
- 1 ½ tsp. ground celery seed
- ½ tsp. cayenne pepper

Directions

1. With a mortar and pestle, or in a coffee grinder, pulverize the bay leaf and salt together. Transfer mixture to a small bowl.
2. Add remaining ingredients and mix with a whisk.
3. Transfer mixture to a spice jar or other airtight container and label. Rub will maintain its flavor for a year at room temperature and longer if stored in the freezer.
4. **To Use:** Apply rub to raw fish or shellfish at a rate of 2 Tbsp. seasoning per pound of meat. See page 145 for cooking instructions.

BERBERE SEASONING

Makes ¾ cup

Berbere seasoning is Ethiopian in origin and found in many dishes from that country. Sometimes sold in paste form, here this spicy, complex seasoning comes to you as a dry mix, which can be added to all manner of things — sprinkle some on chunks of fresh pineapple! — or used on its own as a dry rub for fish or shrimp.

Ingredients

- 2 Tbsp. chili powder
- 1 Tbsp. ground cayenne pepper
- 1 Tbsp. garlic powder
- 1 Tbsp. onion powder
- 1 Tbsp. ground ginger
- 1 Tbsp. paprika (sweet, not hot)
- 2 tsp. salt
- 1 tsp. fenugreek powder or 1 tsp. ground celery seed + ½ tsp. ground cumin
- 1 tsp. ground coriander
- 1 tsp. cardamom
- ½ tsp. dried basil
- ½ tsp. ground black pepper
- ⅛ tsp. ground cinnamon
- ⅛ tsp. ground cloves

Directions

1. In a small bowl, combine all ingredients and mix with a whisk.
2. Transfer mixture to a spice jar or other airtight container and label. Seasoning blend will maintain its flavor for a year at room temperature and longer if stored in the freezer.
3. **To Use:** If using berbere as a rub, apply to raw fish or shellfish at a rate of 2 Tbsp. seasoning per pound of meat. See page 145 for cooking instructions.

CURRY POWDER

Makes ¼ cup

Curry powder is a British-American invention, designed to standardize the complex range of curries in Middle Eastern and Southeast Asian cuisine. Nowadays, curry powder is regarded as an all-purpose seasoning.

Ingredients

- 2 tsp. onion powder (bust up any lumps)
- 2 tsp. ground turmeric
- 1 tsp. ground fenugreek or 1 tsp. ground celery seed + ½ tsp. ground cumin
- ½ tsp. garam masala (store-bought or homemade from recipe on page 151)
- ½ tsp. ground ginger
- ½ tsp. salt
- ¼ tsp. garlic powder
- ¼ tsp. chili powder
- ⅛ tsp. cayenne pepper (for mild heat; increase up to ½ tsp. for extreme heat)
- ⅛ tsp. ground black pepper

Directions

1. In a small bowl, combine all ingredients and mix with a whisk.
2. Transfer mixture to a spice jar or other airtight container and label. Seasoning blend will maintain its flavor for a year at room temperature and longer if stored in the freezer.

GREEK SEASONING

Makes 6 tablespoons (enough to season 3 pounds of meat or potatoes)

I made many attempts to create a shelf-stable Greek seasoning, but never got the results I wanted until I discovered lemon juice powder. It is powerful good, and well-worth tracking down so you can make this, too!

Ingredients

- 2 Tbsp. lemon juice powder (available from many retailers or online)
- 1 Tbsp. garlic powder
- 1 Tbsp. salt
- 1 ½ tsp. dried basil
- 1 tsp. onion powder
- 1 tsp. dried parsley
- 1 tsp. dried lemon peel
- ½ tsp. dried oregano
- ½ tsp. dried marjoram
- ¼ tsp. dried thyme
- ¼ tsp. ground black pepper

Directions

1. In a small bowl, combine all ingredients and mix with a whisk.
2. Transfer mixture to a spice jar or other airtight container and label. Seasoning blend will maintain its flavor for a year at room temperature and longer if stored in the freezer.

To Use:

- **On Vegetables:** Toss diced potatoes or raw vegetables with olive oil and then sprinkle them liberally with seasoning blend. Stir gently and then cook by roasting, steaming, or microwaving.
- **On Meat:** Use seasoning on seafood or meat substitutes by applying before cooking at a rate of 2 Tbsp. seasoning per pound of meat.
- **On Salads:** Make a vinaigrette from ⅔ cup olive oil + ⅓ cup wine vinegar + 3 Tbsp. Greek seasoning blend + 1 Tbsp. brown or Dijon-style mustard. Whisk together to emulsify. Cover and refrigerate for one hour for flavors to develop and blend. Use as a salad dressing or marinade.

ITALIAN SEASONING

Makes 7 tablespoons (enough to season 3 ½ pounds of meat or 3 pounds of potatoes)

I use this stuff on and in everything — veggie burgers, potatoes, vegetables, vinaigrettes — even sprinkled on tossed salads.

Ingredients

- 3 Tbsp. onion powder
- 1 Tbsp. garlic powder
- 1 Tbsp. dried basil
- 2 tsp. dried thyme
- 1 tsp. dried oregano
- 1 tsp. dried, ground rosemary
- 1 tsp. dried parsley
- 1 tsp. salt
- ¼ tsp. ground black pepper

Directions

1. In a small bowl, combine all ingredients and mix with a whisk.
2. Transfer mixture to a spice jar or other airtight container and label. Seasoning blend will maintain its flavor for a year at room temperature and longer if stored in the freezer.

To Use:

- **On Vegetables:** Toss diced potatoes or raw vegetables with olive oil and then sprinkle them liberally with seasoning blend. Stir gently and then cook by roasting, steaming, or microwaving.
- **On Meat:** Use seasoning on seafood or meat substitutes by applying before cooking at a rate of 2 Tbsp. seasoning per pound of meat.
- **On Salads:** Make a vinaigrette from ⅔ cup olive oil + ⅓ cup wine vinegar + 1 Tbsp. balsamic vinegar + 3 Tbsp. Italian seasoning blend + 1 Tbsp. brown or Dijon-style mustard. Whisk together to emulsify. Cover and refrigerate for one hour for flavors to develop and blend. Use as a salad dressing or marinade.

SEASONED SALT
Makes ⅓ cup

Store-bought seasoned salt is certainly convenient, but it is also high in sugar, which I dislike. Therefore, I concocted this delicious homemade version, which relies on seasonings instead of sugar to make things taste yummy. Use in place of salt to season meats, eggs, and vegetables.

Ingredients

- ¼ cup salt
- 1 Tbsp. paprika (sweet, not hot)
- 1 tsp. onion powder
- 1 tsp. garlic powder
- ½ tsp. ground celery seed
- ¼ tsp. ground turmeric
- ¼ tsp. ground black pepper

Directions

1. In a small bowl, combine all ingredients and mix with a whisk.
2. Transfer mixture to a spice jar or jar with a shaker top and label. Seasoning blend will maintain its flavor for a year at room temperature.

SIMON AND GARFUNKEL SEASONING
Makes 4 tablespoons (enough to season 2 pounds of seafood or meat substitutes)

Inspired by the Simon and Garfunkel hit song "Scarborough Fair" with the lyric "parsley, sage, rosemary, and thyme," this spice blend is extremely versatile.

Ingredients

- 1 Tbsp. dried parsley
- 1 Tbsp. dried rosemary
- 1 Tbsp. dried thyme (leaves or ground)
- 1 tsp. dried sage
- 1 tsp. dried basil
- 1 tsp. salt
- 1 tsp. black pepper

Directions

1. In a small bowl, combine all ingredients and mix with a whisk.
2. Transfer mixture to a spice jar or other airtight container and label. Seasoning blend will maintain its flavor for a year at room temperature and longer if stored in the freezer.

To Use:

- **On Vegetables:** Toss diced potatoes or raw vegetables with olive oil and then sprinkle them liberally with seasoning blend. Stir gently and then cook by roasting, steaming, or microwaving.
- **On Meat:** This seasoning activates in fat, so rub raw seafood or meat substitutes with olive or vegetable oil. Then apply seasoning at a rate of 2 Tbsp. seasoning per pound of meat before cooking.

GARAM MASALA
Makes ¼ cup

Garam Masala is a spice blend most common to Indian cooking.

Ingredients

- 1 Tbsp. coriander
- 1 Tbsp. cardamom
- 2 tsp. cumin
- 2 tsp. ground cinnamon
- 1 tsp. black pepper

Directions

1. In a small bowl, combine all ingredients and mix with a whisk.
2. Transfer mixture to a spice jar or other airtight container and label.
3. Seasoning blend will maintain its flavor for a year at room temperature and longer if stored in the freezer.

TACO SEASONING
Makes 7 tablespoons
(equivalent to two store-bought packets)

This is so much better than the store-bought kind, and so much better for you! I started making my own after I actually read the ingredients on one of those packets — so many chemicals in there I nearly got cancer just from reading it. I make this seasoning mix in big batches (double or triple this recipe), so I always have it on hand.

Ingredients

- 2 Tbsp. chili powder
- 1 Tbsp. onion powder
- 1 Tbsp. ground cumin
- 1 Tbsp. salt
- 2 tsp. paprika (sweet, hot, or smoked – your choice)
- 1 tsp. garlic powder
- 1 tsp. dried oregano
- 1 tsp. ground black pepper
- ½ tsp. ground coriander
- ¼ tsp. cayenne pepper (omit if making this for children)

Directions

1. In a small bowl, combine all ingredients and mix with a whisk.
2. Transfer mixture to a spice jar or other airtight container and label.
3. Seasoning blend will maintain its flavor for a year at room temperature and longer if stored in the freezer.

To Use:

- Add 3 Tbsp. seasoning mix to a 12 oz. package of soy veggie crumbles that have been browned in 2 Tbsp. olive or vegetable oil. Stir seasoning in and add ½ to ¾ cup water. Simmer on low heat until liquid has evaporated and seasoning has been absorbed. Stir occasionally.

SALAD DRESSINGS

I was stumped. In a conversation with Aunt Sallie, I mentioned this: What on Earth can I say about salad dressing? Her reply? "Don't you have a funny story about something oily?"

Turns out, I do.

When my oldest son was about 10 months old, there came a day when I needed to pee (every new mother's nightmare). I left him playing happily in the living room, and hurried. I came back moments later to find my son not in the living room, but in the kitchen, completely covered in vegetable oil. He had crawled in, un-done a childproof latch on a lower cupboard, removed a nearly-full bottle of oil, uncapped it (one of those that have to be depressed while turning, no less), and poured said oil all over himself and the floor. He was giddy with delight. It was all SO SLIPPERY! Of course, the only way to clean up the mess involved crossing the kitchen and joining him on his indoor Slip-N-Slide.

You may be wondering what, pray tell, is this story doing in a cookbook? Well, it is reminding you to check your paper towel supply, and it is telling you that vegetable oil (and salad dressing by association) is fun.

AVOCADO SALAD DRESSING
Makes 2 ½ cups

Rich, thick, and creamy, this dressing is not only great on a green salad, but also as a dip for raw veggies.

Ingredients

- 2 large avocados (1 ½ cups)
- 1 small clove garlic (1 scant tsp.)
- 1 green onion, roughly sliced (¼ cup)
- ¼ cup olive oil
- ¼ cup mayonnaise
- ¼ cup sour cream, plain yogurt, or plain Greek yogurt
- ¼ cup buttermilk
- 1 Tbsp. balsamic vinegar
- 2 tsp. lemon juice
- ½ tsp. dill weed
- ½ tsp. granulated sugar
- ½ tsp. salt

Directions

1. Cut avocados in half (top to bottom). Remove pits and scoop flesh into a blender or food processor fitted with a steel blade. Remove and discard any bruises or brown spots as you go.
2. Add remaining ingredients to avocados.
3. Process on low speed until smooth. If dressing is too thick, add a splash of buttermilk and pulse in.
4. Taste, and adjust seasonings.
5. Transfer dressing to a covered bowl or jar and refrigerate until needed. Flavor is best after one hour (flavors meld). Dressing will keep for 2 weeks.

BASIL VINAIGRETTE
Makes 1 cup

Excellent dressing for a tomato-and-fresh-mozzarella Caprese salad, or mixed half-and-half with mayonnaise for a sandwich spread.

Ingredients

- ¾ cup olive oil
- ¼ cup red wine vinegar
- 2 Tbsp. minced fresh basil
- 1 clove garlic, minced and smashed into a paste with 2 pinches salt

Directions

1. Combine all ingredients in a covered jar.
2. Screw lid on tight and shake until ingredients are emulsified. Refrigerate.
3. Vinaigrette will keep for 6 months.

BLEU CHEESE SALAD DRESSING
Makes 1 heaping cup

This salad dressing is rich and delicious, plus quick and easy to make. It is the dressing of choice for the Crab Cobb Salad on page 28, and is also great as a dipping sauce for fresh veggies.

Ingredients

- ½ cup mayonnaise (do not substitute Miracle Whip)
- ¼ cup buttermilk
- 1 tsp. rice wine or white wine vinegar
- 2 pinches salt
- 2 oz. crumbled bleu cheese (½ cup)

Directions

1. In a small bowl or covered jar, combine mayonnaise, buttermilk, vinegar, and salt.
2. Mix with a small whisk or fork until smooth.
3. Add crumbled cheese and blend in. Dressing should be chunky.
4. Cover and refrigerate until needed. Dressing will keep for one month.

CAESAR SALAD DRESSING
Makes 1 cup

This dressing is garlic-y and robust. I use it for all kinds of things from dressing a Caesar salad to marinating fish to saucing sautéed shrimp.

Ingredients

- 6 cloves garlic, sliced (2 Tbsp.)
- 2 Tbsp. mayonnaise
- 1 Tbsp. brown or Dijon-style mustard
- 1 Tbsp. anchovy paste
- 3 Tbsp. lemon juice
- 1 Tbsp. red wine vinegar
- ½ cup olive oil
- ¼ cup grated Parmesan cheese
- salt and black pepper to taste

Directions

1. In container of blender or food processor, dump garlic, mayonnaise, mustard, anchovy paste, lemon juice, and vinegar. Blend on low speed until no chunks of garlic remain.
2. With blender running, add oil in a slow stream.
3. Add cheese and pulse to mix in.
4. Taste, adjust seasonings, and transfer dressing to a covered bowl or jar. Refrigerate until needed. Caesar Dressing will keep for one month.

CRANBERRY-LEMON VINAIGRETTE
Makes 2 ½ cups

Fantastico! Sweet and tart and just heavenly on a tossed salad (especially one topped with goat cheese, walnuts, and pear slices). Well worth the trouble of messing with the cranberries!

Ingredients

- 10 oz. bag frozen cranberries
- ¼ cup water
- ½ cup lemon juice
- 3 Tbsp. olive oil
- 3 Tbsp. white balsamic vinegar
- 4 Tbsp. honey
- 1 Tbsp. brown or Dijon-style mustard
- ½ tsp. salt

Directions

1. **For Cranberries:** In a small saucepan, combine cranberries and water. Cover and place over medium heat.
2. Bring cranberries to a boil. Reduce heat to lowest possible setting and simmer for 20 minutes.
3. Remove from heat. Place a small strainer over a small mixing bowl. Press cranberry mixture through the strainer. Discard skins and bits left in strainer.
4. Add remaining ingredients to cranberry pulp in mixing bowl. Whisk until smooth.
5. Transfer vinaigrette to a covered bowl or jar and refrigerate until needed. Vinaigrette will keep for 3 months.

GREEK VINAIGRETTE
Makes 2 ¼ cups

This vinaigrette is great on tossed salad, pasta salad, chik'n, or in place of plain oil for oven-roasted potatoes. It is also the dressing of choice for the Greek Tortellini Pasta Salad on page 29.

Ingredients

- 1 large green onion, roughly sliced (¼ cup)
- 4 large garlic cloves (4 tsp.)
- ¼ cup crumbled feta cheese (2 oz.)
- ½ cup lemon juice
- ¼ cup red wine vinegar
- ¼ cup balsamic vinegar
- 2 tsp. dried basil
- 1 tsp. dried oregano
- ½ tsp. dried thyme
- 1 tsp. salt
- Pinch black pepper
- 1 cup olive oil

Directions

1. Combine all ingredients except oil in a blender or food processor fitted with a steel blade.
2. Blend on low speed until smooth.
3. With blender running on low, add oil in a steady stream.
4. Taste, adjust seasonings, and transfer vinaigrette to a covered bowl or jar. Refrigerate until needed. Vinaigrette will keep for 6 months.

ITALIAN VINAIGRETTE
Makes 1 ½ cups

This is SO MUCH better than the bottled stuff! For starters, this has no sugar in it (thus making it low-calorie by comparison) and for enders, it is packed with herb-y goodness! Great on just about everything, it is also the dressing of choice for the Pasta Salad on page 138.

Ingredients

- 3 large cloves garlic (1 Tbsp.), minced and smashed into a paste with ½ tsp. salt
- 2 Tbsp. grated Parmesan cheese
- 1 Tbsp. onion powder (bust up any lumps)
- 1 Tbsp. dried parsley
- 1 tsp. dried basil
- ¼ tsp. dried oregano
- ¼ tsp. ground black pepper
- ¾ cup extra virgin olive oil
- ¼ cup red wine vinegar
- 1 Tbsp. balsamic vinegar
- 2 tsp. brown or Dijon-style mustard
- 2 tsp. lemon juice

Directions

1. In a pint jar with a tight-fitting lid, dump all ingredients.
2. Screw on cap and shake vigorously, until ingredients are fully combined and emulsified. Flavor is best after vinaigrette sits with itself for a couple of hours.
3. Store in refrigerator until needed. Vinaigrette will keep for 12 months.

LEMON VINAIGRETTE

Makes ¾ cup

Light and bright, this quick vinaigrette is a refreshing alternative to all those creamy salad dressings. For variety, substitute 1 Tbsp. grated fresh ginger for the clove of garlic.

Ingredients

- 3 Tbsp. fresh lemon juice (1 – 2 lemons)
- 1 large clove garlic (1 tsp.), minced and smashed into a paste with 1 tsp. salt
- 1 tsp. brown or Dijon-style mustard
- 1 tsp. granulated sugar
- 6 Tbsp. olive oil
- 2 Tbsp. snipped fresh chives

Directions

1. In a small mixing bowl, whisk together juice, garlic paste, mustard, and sugar.
2. Slowly add oil while whisking.
3. Stir in chives. Transfer to a covered bowl or jar and refrigerate until needed. Vinaigrette will keep for 6 months.

RANCH SALAD DRESSING

Makes 2 cups

Put this on everything! Fantastic as a salad dressing, dipping sauce for raw vegetables, topping for roasted potatoes, or dipping sauce for fried just-about-anything.

Ingredients

- 1 cup mayonnaise
- ½ cup sour cream
- ½ cup buttermilk
- 1 Tbsp. dried parsley
- 1 tsp. onion powder
- 1 tsp. garlic powder or 1 large clove garlic, minced and smashed to a paste with the salt
- 1 tsp. dill weed
- ½ tsp. salt

Directions

1. In small mixing bowl, combine all ingredients.
2. Stir with a whisk or fork until thoroughly combined.
3. Transfer dressing to a covered bowl or jar and refrigerate until needed. Dressing will keep for 6 months.

RASPBERRY VINAIGRETTE

Makes 1 ¼ cups

A great low-fat dressing for tossed salad, it is the dressing of choice for the Smoked Salmon and Goat Cheese Salad on page 30.

Ingredients

- 1 cup pomegranate juice, simmered until reduced to ½ cup
- 2 Tbsp. olive oil
- 2 Tbsp. rice wine vinegar
- 2 tsp. brown or Dijon-style mustard
- 2 tsp. honey
- 1 tsp. white wine balsamic vinegar
- 1 cup raspberries (fresh or frozen)
- salt and pepper to taste

Directions

1. Place all ingredients in a blender or food processor fitted with a steel blade.
2. Process on low speed until berries are pulverized and mixture is smooth. Taste and adjust seasonings.
3. Transfer vinaigrette to a covered bowl or jar and refrigerate until needed. Vinaigrette will keep for 3 months.

THAI GINGER VINAIGRETTE

Makes 2 cups

I created this vinaigrette to dress a side salad when I was making the Stir-Fry With Spicy Peanut Sauce (recipe on page 117) for dinner. Simply smashing, I make this dressing now whenever we're having salad with any Asian or Asian-inspired main dish. It is also the dressing of choice for the Thai Cold Noodle Salad on page 32.

Ingredients

- 1 Tbsp. grated fresh ginger (peel and grate on a microplane or the finest side of a box grater) or 1 tsp. ground ginger
- 4 green onions, roughly chopped or ½ cup diced red onion
- 1 large clove garlic, sliced (1 tsp.)
- 1 Tbsp. fresh cilantro, roughly chopped
- 1 Tbsp. peanut butter
- 1 Tbsp. bottled fish sauce
- ¼ cup fresh lime juice (2 limes)
- ¼ cup rice wine vinegar
- 1 tsp. granulated sugar
- ½ tsp. salt
- ½ tsp. dried ground ginger
- ¼ tsp. red pepper flakes
- ½ cup vegetable oil
- ¼ cup sesame oil

Directions

1. In the container of a blender or food processor (fitted with a steel blade), combine all ingredients except oils.
2. Process on low speed until smooth and emulsified.
3. Add oils in a slow stream while blender is running.
4. Taste, and adjust seasonings.
5. Transfer vinaigrette to a covered bowl or jar and refrigerate until needed. Vinaigrette will keep for one month.

THOUSAND ISLAND SALAD DRESSING

Makes 1 ½ cups

Great on a tossed salad, as a spread for submarine sandwiches, or as a condiment for veggie burgers.

Ingredients

- 1 large, hard-boiled egg, peeled and pressed through a sieve (instructions for hard boiling on page 3, if needed)
- ¾ cup mayonnaise
- ¼ cup ketchup
- ¼ cup sweet pickle relish
- 1 Tbsp. finely minced white or yellow onion
- 1 dash Tabasco-style hot pepper sauce
- Pinch salt and pepper

Directions

1. In a small mixing bowl, combine all ingredients.
2. Mix with a whisk until smooth and emulsified. Taste and adjust seasonings.
3. Transfer dressing to a covered bowl or jar and refrigerate until needed. Dressing will keep for 3 months.

DIPPING SAUCES

My earliest recollection of employing a dipping sauce was at Red Lobster when I was about ten. I was indulging in crab legs for the first time and dipping beautiful, succulent chunks of crab meat in melted butter. I was in heaven. I may, or may not have ruined my outfit, despite the employment of a lobster bib, but I did not care. That meal was amazing.

The dipping sauce recipes in this chapter are a bit more involved than simply "melt butter," but their purpose is the same — to elevate a dish from earthly good to heavenly divine.

CILANTRO PESTO
Makes 1 ½ cups

I use this pesto as a dipping sauce for a variety of Mexican foods and to "dress up" all sorts of things like quesadillas and refried beans.

Ingredients

- 2 cups cilantro leaves and small stems (1 bunch from grocery store)
- 3 large garlic cloves, sliced (1 Tbsp.)
- 1 jalapeño, seeded and roughly diced (leave seeds in for a hotter pesto)
- ¼ cup sunflower seeds
- ½ tsp. ground cumin
- ¼ tsp. salt
- ½ cup sesame oil
- ¼ cup vegetable oil
- 1 Tbsp. lime juice (½ lime)
- ½ cup grated Asiago cheese (2 oz.)

Directions

1. In container of blender or food processor fitted with a steel blade, dump all ingredients except cheese.
2. Pulse mixture a few times to begin to chop leaves. Pack cilantro leaves down in-between pulsings.
3. Once mixture begins to blend, process it on high until the cilantro is finely ground and the mixture is emulsified.
4. Add cheese and pulse a few times to mix in.
5. Taste, and adjust seasonings.
6. If not using cilantro pesto right away, freeze it in an ice cube tray. Once frozen, transfer cubes to a ziptop bag and remove them to thaw as needed. Pesto will keep in the freezer for one year.

CHIPOTLE AIOLI
Makes 1 cup

This spicy aioli is great as a dipping sauce for empanadas and quesadillas, or as a spread on sandwiches.

Ingredients

- 1 egg yolk (organic, if at all possible)
- 1 tsp. brown or Dijon-style mustard
- ½ cup vegetable oil
- ¼ cup olive oil
- 1 small clove garlic (1 scant tsp.), minced and smashed to a paste with ¼ tsp. salt
- 1 Tbsp. chipotle peppers in adobo sauce, finely minced (¼ of a 4 oz. can – chop and freeze the rest of the can, for a later use)
- 2 tsp. balsamic vinegar
- ½ tsp. ground coriander

Directions

1. In small bowl, whisk egg yolk and mustard together.
2. Dribble in small bits of oil at a time, whisking vigorously after each addition until all the oil is fully incorporated into the egg yolk mixture.
3. Add remaining ingredients and mix in.
4. Transfer aioli to a covered container and refrigerate. Aioli will keep for several weeks.

HOISIN SAUCE
Makes 1 cup

This sauce has a kick to it — perfect as a dipping sauce for most any Asian dumpling!

Ingredients

- 1 large clove garlic, finely minced or pressed (1 tsp.)
- 3 Tbsp. brown sugar
- 3 Tbsp. soy sauce
- 3 Tbsp. rice wine vinegar
- 2 Tbsp. Chinese black bean sauce (fermented black soy beans) + 2 Tbsp. water or 4 Tbsp. miso + 2 Tbsp. water or 4 Tbsp. natural peanut butter + 2 Tbsp. molasses
- 2 tsp. Sriracha hot sauce or Chinese hot sauce (adds medium heat to sauce; for a mild sauce, use ½ tsp.)
- 1 ½ tsp. sesame oil
- ½ tsp. Chinese five-spice powder (cinnamon, anise, fennel, ginger, clove, and licorice root)
- ¼ tsp. ground black pepper

Directions

1. In a 1-quart saucepan, combine all sauce ingredients.
2. Place pot over medium-high heat and cover. Bring sauce to a boil, stirring often.
3. Reduce heat to low and simmer for 5 minutes, stirring often.
4. Remove from heat and allow to cool. Transfer to a covered container and refrigerate. Hoisin Sauce will keep for six months.

PESTO SAUCE
Makes 2 cups

The roasted garlic in this recipe gives the finished pesto a smooth instead of sharp garlic flavor. If you like your pesto sharp, add one clove of fresh garlic to the mix.

Ingredients

Garlic:

- 1 head garlic
- 1 tsp. olive oil

Pesto:

- 6 cups fresh basil leaves (lightly packed)
- ½ cup pine nuts or pumpkin seeds
- 1 tsp. salt
- ½ tsp. lemon juice
- 2 cups finely grated fresh Parmesan, Romano, or Asiago cheese
- 1 cup extra virgin olive oil

Directions

1. **For Garlic:** preheat oven (or toaster oven) to 375°.
2. Set head of garlic on a 6" (give or take) square of aluminum foil. Drizzle teaspoon of oil over the garlic.
3. Bring the aluminum foil up and around the garlic and twist everything together at the top to seal the garlic in.
4. Roast garlic for 40 minutes.
5. **For Pesto:** In the container of a blender or food processor fitted with a metal blade, combine 4 cups of basil leaves, nuts, salt, and lemon juice.
6. Process on high until basil is finely chopped.
7. Add remaining basil leaves, Parmesan cheese, and olive oil. Pop the garlic cloves out of their papery skins and add all of the cloves to the basil mixture.
8. Process mixture on high until basil pieces are tiny and the oil is emulsified into the mixture. Taste and adjust seasonings as needed.
9. Store pesto in a covered container in the refrigerator (top mixture with a teaspoon or two of olive oil to prevent the surface from browning), or freeze mixture in an ice cube tray. Once frozen, transfer cubes of pesto to a ziptop bag. Pesto will keep in the refrigerator for several weeks, or in the freezer for a year.

PIZZA SAUCE
Makes 4 cups

Made from pantry staples, this sauce is great as a dipping sauce for calzones or as the sauce on a standard pizza. Quick to make and fresher-tasting than store-bought!

Ingredients

- 1 Tbsp. olive oil
- 1 Tbsp. finely minced or pressed garlic (3 large cloves)
- 1 Tbsp. onion powder
- 2 tsp. dried basil
- ½ tsp. dried oregano
- ⅛ tsp. red pepper flakes
- 14 oz. can crushed tomatoes (2 cups)
- 6 oz. can tomato paste (⅓ cup)
- ½ tsp. granulated sugar
- ½ tsp. salt

Directions

1. In a 1-quart saucepan, heat oil over medium heat.
2. When oil is hot, add garlic, onion powder, basil, oregano, and pepper flakes. Stir.
3. Immediately add tomatoes, paste, sugar, and salt. Stir.
4. Heat sauce to boiling (do not cover). Stir, reduce heat to low, and simmer sauce for 5 minutes, stirring occasionally.
5. Remove sauce from heat and allow to cool. Extra sauce may be kept in the refrigerator for 1 week or in an airtight container(s) in the freezer for up to 1 year.

SALSA VERDE
Makes 1 ½ cups

If you have a garden, you can make this with green, unripe tomatoes in place of the tomatillos. Tangy, hot, sweet, creamy — this salsa has it all! Great on just about any Mexican dish, this salsa also complements scrambled eggs and baked fish.

Ingredients

- 1 large, ripe avocado (1 cup flesh)
- ¾ cup diced tomatillos (4 – 6 fruits; let ripen at room temperature until papery covering is dry, remove covering and wash sticky substance off fruits)
- 4 oz. can mild, diced green chile peppers
- ¼ cup finely minced white or yellow onion
- ½ jalapeño pepper, finely minced with seeds left in (use the whole jalapeño for hotter salsa)
- 2 Tbsp. finely minced fresh cilantro leaves
- 1 tsp. minced garlic (1 large clove), smashed to a paste with ¼ tsp. salt
- 1 Tbsp. vegetable oil
- 1 Tbsp. lime juice (½ of a lime)
- 1 tsp. agave or granulated sugar

Directions

1. Cut avocado in half top-to-bottom, remove pit, and scoop flesh into a small mixing bowl. Remove any bruises or brown spots as you go. Mash avocado flesh with a fork.
2. Add remaining ingredients to bowl. Stir until well mixed.
3. Taste, and adjust seasonings.
4. Transfer salsa to a covered container and refrigerate until needed. Salsa may be made up to 3 days before serving.

SWEET-AND-SOUR SAUCE #1
Makes 1 cup

Easy peasy! And great as a dipping sauce for egg rolls, dumplings, or fried fish.

Ingredients

- ¼ cup soy sauce
- ¼ cup rice wine vinegar
- ¼ cup honey
- ¼ cup ketchup

Directions

1. In a small bowl, combine all ingredients.
2. Stir with a fork or whisk until thoroughly blended. Cover and refrigerate until needed. Sweet-and-Sour Sauce will keep for 6 months.

SKORDALIA
Makes 1 ½ cups

Skordalia is a thick garlic sauce of Greek origin, commonly served with batter-fried fish or fried vegetables. This sauce is definitely a garlic-lover's dream and a garlic-haters nightmare, so plan accordingly!

Ingredients

- 14 oz. can potatoes, drained
- 6 large cloves garlic, sliced (2 Tbsp.)
- ½ cup olive oil
- ¼ cup white wine vinegar
- 1 tsp. lemon juice
- ½ tsp. salt

Directions

1. In the container of a blender or food processor fitted with a steel blade, add all ingredients. Process until mixture is smooth and emulsified.
2. Transfer skordalia to a covered container and refrigerate until needed. Skordalia will keep for one week.

SWEET-AND-SOUR SAUCE #2
Makes 1 cup

Thick and flavorful, this sweet-and-sour sauce is more complicated to make and more complex in its flavor profile than Sauce #1.

Ingredients

- 1 Tbsp. vegetable oil
- 1 Tbsp. sesame oil
- 1 Tbsp. grated fresh ginger (peel, then grate on a microplane or the finest side of a box grater) or 1 tsp. ground ginger
- 2 cloves garlic, finely minced or pressed (2 tsp.)
- ¼ cup brown sugar
- ¼ cup soy sauce
- ¼ cup rice wine vinegar
- 1 Tbsp. ketchup
- ¼ tsp. dried ginger
- 1 Tbsp. cornstarch
- 1 Tbsp. water

Directions

1. This sauce cooks very quickly, so have all ingredients at hand before you begin.
2. In small saucepan, heat oils over medium heat.
3. Add fresh ginger and garlic. Sauté 30 seconds, stirring constantly.
4. Add sugar, soy sauce, vinegar, ketchup, and dried ginger. Stir.
5. In a small ramekin or tiny bowl, combine the cornstarch and water. Stir well, scraping the bottom of the bowl to dissolve all of the cornstarch.
6. When mixture in pot comes to a boil, add cornstarch mixture to thicken sauce. Cook one minute, stirring constantly.
7. Remove from heat and allow to cool. Store in a covered container in the refrigerator. Sweet-and-Sour Sauce will keep for 6 months.

TARTAR SAUCE
Makes ¾ cup

A classic! Perfect on any fishy sandwich or as a dipping sauce for fried fish or shrimp.

Ingredients

- ½ cup mayonnaise
- ¼ cup dill pickle relish
- ¼ cup finely minced green onion (1 onion)
- 2 tsp. yellow mustard
- 2 tsp. capers, finely minced

Directions

1. In a small bowl or covered container, combine all ingredients.
2. Stir with a whisk or fork until homogenous. Cover and refrigerate until needed. Tartar Sauce will keep for 6 months.

TOUM
Makes ⅓ cup

Toum is a mayonnaise-like garlic sauce of Mediterranean origins. Extremely versatile, it is a classic condiment for falafel. I love it on burgers and sandwiches, too.

Ingredients

- 1 large clove garlic (1 tsp.), finely minced and smashed into a paste with ⅛ tsp. salt
- 2 Tbsp. plain Greek yogurt or sour cream
- 1 tsp. lemon juice
- 1 tsp. ice water
- 2 Tbsp. canola oil

Directions

1. Place garlic, yogurt, lemon juice, and water in a mug or small bowl.
2. Whisk until smooth and emulsified.
3. Add the oil and whisk vigorously.
4. Transfer to a covered container and chill until serving time. Toum will keep for one month.

TZATZIKI SAUCE
Makes 1 ½ cups

This stuff is soooo gooooood! Tzatziki Sauce is the perfect dipping sauce for all things Greek and Middle Eastern: falafel, dolmades, Greek meatballs, and spanakopita. Fresh and tangy, it is also great on burgers and sandwiches — especially in combination with feta cheese.

Ingredients

- 1 cup plain Greek yogurt
- 1 cup cucumber, peeled, grated, and drained (put in a strainer and press the moisture out)
- 1 large clove garlic (1 tsp.), finely minced and smashed to a paste with ½ tsp. salt
- ⅛ tsp. black pepper
- Pinch of sugar
- 1 Tbsp. olive oil
- 1 Tbsp. white wine vinegar

Directions

1. In a small bowl, combine all ingredients. Whisk until emulsified.
2. Transfer to a covered container and refrigerate at least 1 hour before serving. Tzatziki will keep for 2 weeks.

ARTICHOKE DIPPING SAUCE

Makes enough for 2 large artichokes

This is a fantastic dipping sauce to accompany cooked artichokes. Serve the sauce in small ramekins so each person has their own "pot" to dip leaves in.

Ingredients

- 1 Tbsp. olive oil
- 1 Tbsp. brown or Dijon-style mustard
- 2 tsp. red wine vinegar
- 1 tsp. lemon juice

Directions

1. In a small, covered jar, combine ingredients. Shake until emulsified.
2. Refrigerate until needed. Sauce will keep for one year.

SEAFOOD COCKTAIL SAUCE

Makes ½ cup

I love this as a dipping sauce for lots of things: shrimp, fried fish, and pigs-n-blankets, to name a few.

Ingredients

- ¼ cup ketchup
- ¼ cup brown or Dijon-style mustard
- 4 tsp. prepared horseradish

Directions

1. In a small bowl or covered container, combine all ingredients.
2. Stir until thoroughly blended.
3. Cover and refrigerate until needed. Seafood Cocktail Sauce will keep for one year.

INDEX

A
APPETIZERS
Coconut Shrimp, 81
Crab Deviled Eggs, 3
Crab Egg Rolls, 83
Salmon Ceviche, 73
Salmon Patties, 42

B
BLACK BEANS
30-Minute Chili, 54
Black Bean Burrito Bowls, 97
Brazilian Feijoada, 14
Breakfast Burrito, 2
Chili, 15
Mexican Grain Salad, 136
Nut Burgers, 41
Salsa Beans, 112
Spicy Black Bean Burgers, 44
Taco Casserole, 112
Tex-Mex Breakfast Casserole, 12

BREAKFAST
Biscuits and Sausage Gravy, 96
Breakfast Burrito, 2
Creamed Spinach with Eggs on Top, 4
Egg Casserole with Cheese Sauce, 5
"Ham"-and-Egg Cups, 7
Quiche, 8
Shakshuka, 10
Strata, 11
Tex-Mex Breakfast Casserole, 12

BURGERS
Lentil Burgers, 40
Cram Cakes, 36
Nut Burgers, 41
Salmon Patties, 42
Spicy Black Bean Burgers, 44

C
CHICKPEAS
Falafel, 39
Nut Burgers, 41
Spicy Black Bean Burgers, 44
Tabbouleh Salad with Shrimp, 31

CHIK'N
Brazilian Feijoada, 14
Calzones, 48
Chik'n Caesar Wrap, 34
Chik'n Pot Pie, 98
Creamy Chik'n Noodle Soup, 16
Greek Tortellini Pasta Salad, 29
Gumbo, 17
Pasta Salad, 138
Tabbouleh Salad with Shrimp, 31
Tarascan Indian Soup, 25

CLAM JUICE
Clams in White Sauce with Linguini, 80
Cram Cakes, 36
Lobster Mac-N-Cheese, 86
Mussels, 87
Seafood Chowder, 21
Seafood Newburg, 89
Smoked Salmon Stew, 22
Tuscan Stuffed Mahi Mahi, 78

CLAMS
Clams in White Sauce with Linguini, 80
Cram Cakes, 36
Seafood Chowder, 21

CRAB
Crab Cobb Salad, 28
Crab Deviled Eggs, 3
Crab Egg Rolls, 83
Crab Quiche, 84
Crab Wrap, 35
Cram Cakes, 36
Lobster Mac-N-Cheese, 86
Quiche, 9
Seafood Chowder, 21
Seafood Lasagna, 90
Seafood Newburg, 89
Seafood Salad, 43
Tilapia Stuffed with Lobster, 77

D
DIPPING SAUCES
Artichoke Dipping Sauce, 164
Chipotle Aioli, 159
Cilantro Pesto, 159
Hoisin Sauce, 160
Pesto Sauce, 160
Pizza Sauce, 161
Salsa Verde, 161
Seafood Cocktail Sauce, 164
Skordalia, 162
Sweet-and-Sour Sauce #1, 162
Sweet-and-Sour Sauce #2, 162

Tartar Sauce, 163
Toum, 163
Tzatziki Sauce, 163

F
FISH
Baked Lemon-Garlic Fish, 55
Beer Battered Fish, 66
Fish Curry, 67
Fish Sticks, 70
Fish Tacos with Kimchi Slaw, 68
Fried Fish Sandwich, 37
Swordfish Kebabs, 76
Tilapia Stuffed with Lobster, 77
Tuscan Stuffed Mahi Mahi, 78

FISH STOCK
Lobster Mac-N-Cheese, 86
Mussels, 87
Seafood Chowder, 21
Seafood Newburg, 89
Smoked Salmon Stew, 22
Tuscan Stuffed Mahi Mahi, 78

L
LENTILS
Lentil-Barley Stew, 19
Lentil Burgers, 40
Sloppy Joes, 62
Spicy Lentil Soup, 23

LOBSTER
Lobster Mac-N-Cheese, 86
Seafood Newburg, 89
Tilapia Stuffed with Lobster, 77

LUNCH
Black Bean Burrito Bowls, 97
Chik'n Caesar Wrap, 34
Crab Wrap, 35
Cram Cakes, 36
Egg Salad, 6
Falafel, 38
Fried Fish Sandwich, 37
Lentil Burgers, 40

Nut Burgers, 41
Salmon Patties, 42
Seafood Salad, 43
Spicy Black Bean Burgers, 44

M
MUSSELS
Mussels, 87

N
NAVY BEANS
Mixed Bean Soup, 20
Smoked Salmon Stew, 22
Vegan Baked Beans, 144
White Bean Soup, 26

P
PASTA
Clams in White Sauce with Linguini, 80
Creamy Pesto Orzo with Shrimp, 56
Dolmades (Stuffed Grape Leaves), 114
Greek Tortellini Pasta Salad, 29
Lasagna, 104
Lemon Orzo, 132
Lobster Mac-N-Cheese, 86
Macaroni and Cheese, 106
Mostaccioli, 107
Mussels, 87
Pasta Salad, 138
Quick Macaroni and Cheese, 59
Salmon Alfredo, 72
Scallops and Gnocchi in Cream Sauce, 88
Seafood Lasagna, 90
Spaghetti with Roasted Vegetable Sauce, 116
Stir-Fry with Spicy Peanut Sauce, 117
Stroganoff, 109
Swiss Macaroni and Cheese, 111

Tabbouleh Salad with Shrimp, 31
Thai Cold Noodle Salad, 32
Tony Macaroni, 63
Vegan Macaroni and Cheese, 120

PIZZA
Calzones, 48
Chicago-Style Deep Dish Pizza, 46
Margherita Pizza, 49
Mexican Pizza, 50
Sicilian Pizza, 51
White Pizza, 52

POTATOES
"Ham" and Scalloped Potatoes, 101
Kielbasa and Potatoes, 58
Mashed Potatoes, 134
Potato Salad, 139
Seafood Chowder, 21
Shepherd's Pie, 108
Stroganoff, 109
Swiss Macaroni and Cheese, 111
Tex-Mex Breakfast Casserole, 12

Q
QUINOA
Black Bean Burrito Bowls, 97
Brazilian Feijoada, 14
Indian "Meat" Balls in Coconut Curry Sauce, 102
Indian Stew, 18
Mexican Grain Salad, 136
Quinoa with Raisins and Pepitas, 140
Sweet-and-Sour, 118

R
RICE
Bibimbap, 95
Brazilian Feijoada, 14

Coconut-Lime Shrimp, 82
Fancy Rice, 127
Gumbo, 17
Indian "Meat" Balls in Coconut Curry Sauce, 102
Lentil Burgers, 40
Masala Peanuts, 115
Mexican Rice, 137
Seafood Newburg, 89
Shrimp Fried Rice, 61
Stroganoff, 109
Stuffed Peppers, 110
Sweet-and-Sour, 118
Tuna-Rice Delight, 73

RUBS AND SEASONINGS
Berbere Seasoning, 148
Cajun Rub, 146
Chinese 12-Spice Rub, 146
Curry Powder, 148
Garam Masala, 151
Greek Seasoning, 149
Hot Mustard Rub, 146
Indian Rub, 147
Italian Seasoning, 149
Seasoned Salt, 150
Simon and Garfunkel Seasoning, 150
Taco Seasoning, 151
Texas Rub, 147

S
SALAD DRESSINGS
Avocado Salad Dressing, 153
Basil Vinaigrette, 153
Bleu Cheese Salad Dressing, 153
Caesar Salad Dressing, 154
Cranberry-Lemon Vinaigrette, 154
Greek Vinaigrette, 155
Italian Vinaigrette, 155
Lemon Vinaigrette, 156
Ranch Salad Dressing, 156
Raspberry Vinaigrette, 156
Thai Ginger Vinaigrette, 157
Thousand Island Salad Dressing, 157

SALADS
Crab Cobb Salad, 28
Creamy Coleslaw, 126
Egg Salad, 6
Greek Tortellini Pasta Salad, 29
Mexican Grain Salad, 136
Pasta Salad, 138
Potato Salad, 139
Smoked Salmon and Goat Cheese Salad, 30
Tabbouleh Salad with Shrimp, 31
Thai Cold Noodle Salad, 32

SALMON
Chicago-Style Deep Dish Pizza, 47
Marinated Salmon, 71
Salmon Alfredo, 72
Salmon Ceviche, 73
Salmon Patties, 42
Salmon Quiche, 74
Salmon with Honey-Mustard Glaze, 60
Smoked Salmon and Goat Cheese Salad, 30
Smoked Salmon Stew, 22
Spinach and Feta Stuffed Salmon, 75

SANDWICHES
Chik'n Caesar Wrap, 34
Crab Wrap, 35
Falafel, 38
Fried fish Sandwich, 37
Seafood Salad, 43
Sloppy Joes, 62

SCALLOPS
Scallops and Gnocchi in Cream Sauce, 88
Seafood Chowder, 21
Seafood Newburg, 89

SHRIMP
Calzones, 48
Chicago-Style Deep Dish Pizza, 47
Coconut-Lime Shrimp, 82
Coconut Shrimp, 81
Creamy Pesto Orzo with Shrimp, 56
Garlic Shrimp, 57
Gumbo, 17
Pasta Salad, 138
Quiche, 9
Seafood Chowder, 21
Seafood Lasagna, 90
Seafood Newburg, 89
Seafood Salad, 43
Shrimp Fajitas, 92
Shrimp Fried Rice, 61
Tabbouleh Salad with Shrimp, 31

SIDE DISHES
"Bacon" Onion Rings, 122
Cornbread, 124
Cornbread Stuffing, 123
Creamy Coleslaw, 126
Fancy Rice, 127
Focaccia, 128
Fried Green Tomatoes, 129
Hush Puppies, 130
Irish Soda Bread, 131
Lemon Orzo, 132
Marinated Vegetables, 133
Mashed Potatoes, 134
Mexican Grain Salad, 136
Mexican Rice, 137
Pasta Salad, 138
Potato Salad, 139
Quinoa with Raisins and Pepitas, 140
Refried Beans, 141
Salsa Beans, 112
Scones, 142
Sweet Potato Fries, 140
Thanksgiving Sage-Onion Stuffing, 143
Vegan Baked Beans, 144
Vegan Cornbread, 125

SOUPS
30-Minute Chili, 54
Brazilian Feijoada, 14
Chili, 15

Creamy Chik'n Noodle
  Soup, 16
Gumbo, 17
Mixed Bean Soup, 20
Seafood Chowder, 21
Spicy Lentil Soup, 23
Split Pea Soup, 24
Tarascan Indian Soup, 25
White Bean Soup, 26

SPECIAL OCCASION
Bibimbap, 94
Seafood Lasagna, 90
Seafood Newburg, 89
Swellington Wellington, 119

STEWS
Indian Stew, 18
Lentil-Barley Stew, 19
Smoked Salmon Stew, 22

SWEET POTATOES
Sweet Potato Fries, 140

T

TOFU
Bibimbap, 95
Creamy Chik'n Noodle
  Soup, 16
Stir-Fry with Spicy Peanut
  Sauce, 117
White Bean Soup, 26

TUNA
Thai Cold Noodle Salad, 32
Tuna-Rice Delight, 73
Wasabi Tuna Steaks, 64

V

VEGAN
"Bacon" Onion Rings, 122
Brazilian Feijoada, 14
Dolmades (Stuffed Grape
  Leaves), 114
Fancy Rice, 127
Focaccia, 128

Indian Stew, 18
Lemon Orzo, 132
Lentil-Barley Stew, 19
Marinated Vegetables, 133
Masala Peanuts, 115
Mashed Potatoes, 134
Mexican Rice, 137
Mixed Bean Soup, 20
Nut Burgers, 41
Quinoa with Raisins and
  Pepitas, 140
Spaghetti with Roasted
  Vegetable Sauce, 116
Spicy Lentil Soup, 23
Stir-fry with Spicy Peanut
  Sauce, 117
Sweet-and-Sour, 118
Sweet Potato Fries, 140
Swellington Wellington, 119
Vegan Baked Beans, 144
Vegan Cornbread, 125
Vegan Macaroni and
  Cheese, 120
White Bean Soup, 26

VEGETARIAN
30-Minute Chili, 54
Bibimbap, 94
Biscuits and Sausage Gravy, 96
Black Bean Burrito Bowls, 97
Breakfast Burrito, 2
Calzones, 48
Chik'n Pot Pie, 98
Chik'n Caesar Wrap, 34
Chicago-Style Deep Dish
  Pizza, 46
Chili, 15
Creamed Spinach with Eggs on
  Top, 4
Egg Casserole with Cheese
  Sauce, 5
Egg Salad, 6
Eggplant Parmigiana, 100
Falafel, 38
Greek Tortellini Pasta Salad, 29
"Ham" and Scalloped
  Potatoes, 101
"Ham"-and-Egg Cups, 7

Indian "Meat" Balls in
  Coconut Curry Sauce, 102
Lasagna, 104
Lentil Burgers, 40
Macaroni and Cheese, 59, 106
Margherita Pizza, 49
Mexican Pizza, 50
Mostaccioli, 107
Nut Burgers, 41
Quiche, 8
Salsa Beans, 112
Shakshuka, 10
Shepherd's Pie, 108
Spicy Black Bean Burgers, 44
Sicilian Pizza, 51
Sloppy Joes, 62
Strata, 11
Stroganoff, 109
Stuffed Peppers, 110
Swiss Macaroni and
  Cheese, 111
Taco Casserole, 112
Tex-Mex Breakfast
  Casserole, 12
Tony Macaroni, 63
White Pizza, 52

VEGGIE SOY CRUMBLES
30-Minute Chili, 54
Dolmades (Stuffed Grape
  Leaves), 114
Lasagna, 104
Mostaccioli, 107
Shepherd's Pie, 108
Sloppy Joes, 62
Spaghetti with Roasted
  Vegetable Sauce, 116
Stroganoff, 109
Taco Seasoning, 151
Tex-Mex Breakfast
  Casserole, 12
Tony Macaroni, 63

www.ingramcontent.com/pod-product-compliance
Lightning Source LLC
Chambersburg PA
CBHW040310240426
43666CB00021B/2918